T0368174

PHILIPPIANS

A SELF-GUIDED STUDY FOR INDIVIDUALS OR GROUPS

"THAT I MAY KNOW HIM"

DIANE JUNKER

WESTBOW
PRESS®
A DIVISION OF THOMAS NELSON
& ZONDERVAN

WestBow Press books may be ordered through booksellers or by contacting:

WestBow Press
A Division of Thomas Nelson & Zondervan
1663 Liberty Drive
Bloomington, IN 47403
www.westbowpress.com
844-714-3454

ISBN: 979-8-3850-1922-9 (sc)
ISBN: 979-8-3850-1921-2 (e)

Library of Congress Control Number: 2024903204

Print information available on the last page.

WestBow Press rev. date: 5/1/2024

For Mom and Dad who modeled a life of faith
and love for the Lord and His word.

For my family, friends, and all those at Kensington
Church who journeyed through many Bible studies
with me offering sound advice, prayerful support,
and countless words of encouragement.

For my husband whose unending love
and support made this possible.

Contents

Foreword

Over 30 years ago, I got to be part of a team that started a church to reach people who were either far from God or felt far from God. We found great favor with God and people, and people came from all over to meet the Jesus who loves them and gave Himself for them!!!

Not long after, we realized that thousands were coming who had received the grace and forgiveness offered by Jesus! But at the same time, we realized that they didn't know the Bible, didn't know where to begin, or how to study for themselves. Most of them had rarely, if ever, opened the Bible to experience the truth of God's Word.

As is common, the women of our church were being more proactive, looking for opportunities to grow and deepen in their faith. Lynn Block, our children and family director in the early days, started creating seminars and events for women, but what was needed was a place where women could study the Bible weekly together.

At this point, Diane entered the picture, creating original Bible studies that allowed women to really know the Bible. From the beginning, she has had a remarkable way of writing inductive Bible Studies of books of the Bible, in which women at all stages of their spiritual journey could participate fully. One of DD's hallmarks was "never assume that people have previous knowledge of the Bible." Because of this, her studies took women (and later men, as well) on a journey they could all navigate together. She has been, and is, skilled at writing thought-provoking questions that get people interested in discovering the truths of God's Word.

For 30 years, DD has led a ministry where hundreds and hundreds of women have become dedicated students of the Bible and deeply committed disciples of Jesus. I have personally seen life after life transformed from the Insights Ministry, and a marvelous number of those women are serving Jesus in a thousand different arenas!!

Three things I am most deeply grateful for as Diane's pastor (and brother-in-law):

1) For all the years I've known her, she has been steadfastly growing in her walk with Jesus. There were years when Paula, her sister, and I benefited from DD's advice, and her care for us was critical for getting us through some very difficult early years of marriage.

2) She has modeled openhandedness in her life. She has trained dozens of women to be powerful Bible teachers. People in our community love her and are so grateful for her life, but she remains a normal human like the rest of us, seeking to walk with Jesus on the same ground where we walk. She models for people that you can walk with Jesus for a lifetime.

3) She has truly "done the work". Her diligent study and effort have moved countless people toward discipleship and growing in their understanding of God's truth. She is all

for the Glory of Jesus Christ. In all these years, she led and created as a lay person, never a paid staff person, but a volunteer leader who has been worth millions to us!

I have wanted her to publish materials for many years. What joy for me that this is finally happening!!! May these studies awaken people's hearts to Jesus. Only in Heaven will we know how wonderful this impact will be.

Steve Andrews
Co-founding Pastor Kensington Church

Preface

There are times in our lives when God unexpectedly grabs our attention and speaks into our hearts and minds with a new and surprising understanding of His truth and love. During my early teenage years, I experienced one of those events.

Whenever my three sisters or I struggled with homework, we would usually seek my father's help. The door to his office was always open. Even if he was busy at work and deep in thought, we were free to interrupt. I can still picture his desk with all the papers piled on top and the shelves above it lined with Bibles and other reference books. He loved the Bible and studied it diligently with the precision of an engineer and the heart of a Christ follower. Through the years, God's Word had become more and more a part of his life, and he was always eager to share something he had learned.

Often, when I was asking for help with homework, I would also seek advice about other issues. More often than not, during those discussions, my Dad's hand would reach up to take a Bible down, and somehow he would find just the right verse to address the problem I was struggling with. I remember being amazed at how he could do that!

However, as I grew older, I began to question and challenge the idea that finding answers in God's Word was the best way. I imagined that my opinion was as good as anyone else's opinion, and it was probably as good as what God had to say.

On one occasion, when I wanted to talk to Dad about something "important," I was determined to discuss it without him showing me a Bible verse! During the conversation, I tried to keep him occupied and distracted by asking one question after another as quickly as I could, but my efforts didn't stop him from eventually reaching up to the shelf above lined with Bibles. When I saw his hand bringing one down, I blurted out impatiently, "Dad, I just want to know what *you* think."

He stopped suddenly, paused, and then with a confused look on his face, said gently and quietly, "But this is the only answer I have."

Today I no longer remember what the issue was that I thought was so important, nor do I remember the answer my Dad gave me, but I will always remember walking out of that room thinking, "This is real to Him. He believes that the Bible, God's word, is actually **the** truth and the best answer for life."

That encounter, at a tender age, dramatically changed my perspective and put me on a path that led to my treasuring the words of scripture as life-giving and true. It has been a process of growing and stumbling, often failing to go to the Bible first or follow it faithfully; but whenever I have earnestly sought and heeded God's Word, it has never failed to yield the guidance, comfort, and answers I needed. Best of all, those words of truth led me to know Jesus Christ, the living Word, and to understand His heart of mercy and love. (John 5:39, 46)

∽

My hope and prayer is that, just as my earthly father's hand reached up to open a Bible and lead me to answers and guidance for my life, this study will help you find the guidance and comfort you are seeking. As you open the Bible may you find your heavenly Father's hand reaching out to you with His words of truth to meet your every need and lead you to His grace and peace.

His door is always open. His Word is within reach. His smile and the treasures of His love are waiting for you there.

About this Study Guide

This study guide can be used individually or with a friend or group.

Questions are designed to help discover the meaning of Bible passages by looking at one verse at a time, or one phrase at a time, or even one word at a time. Slowing down and looking at the Bible in smaller portions makes it easier to understand and absorb the material. This can also lead to seeing the larger picture better.

In the main body of the text, **the numbered questions** ask you to **observe** things about the passage you are reading. They examine the "who, what, when, where, why, and how" in the text and help reveal the meaning of the passage.

"Digging Deeper" questions (in boxes on the right) encourage you to compare other portions of scripture and find additional information about the passage. These help with **interpretation** and can also lead to other related topics.

"FYI" inserts are quotes from commentators that explain or expand on what you are studying. There are also word definitions or links to online sites for related information and more research.

"Applying the Word" questions encourage you to **apply** what you have learned to your life.

Suggestions for Small Groups:

Begin with prayer. Read the portion of scripture being covered before starting on the questions. It can be more interesting, especially with limited time, to cover questions that people are most interested in, or issues that they want to discuss, rather than going through the questions sequentially.

During the week, as each person goes through the homework, it is helpful to mark questions they especially want to cover and also write down any additional questions they want to share with their small group.

People should feel free to fill in as much or as little as they want in the spaces provided in the study guide. If a person has a stressful week and can't get to the homework, it is helpful to just read the passage of scripture being covered that week. During small group time, everyone should be encouraged to fill in their unanswered questions or add to their answers as others share.

Often a person's answer may be different than another person's answer. Various viewpoints in understanding and interpretation can lead to discussions that give deeper insights and clarity for everyone involved.

Lessons are divided into four days to break the passage being studied into easier-to-manage portions and allow time to reflect on the truths of God's Word. (For small groups, four days allows for no homework on the day the group meets and two days free.)

Whenever you open up the Bible, you give God the opportunity to meet with you and fill your life with His love and truth. God's Word is His **love letter** to us. It blesses us with His instructions for life—from the One who knows us best!

Scripture can bring refreshment, wisdom, joy, and light into our lives (Psalm 19:7–8). It fills us with encouragement and hope (Romans 15:4); protects (Psalm 18:30); equips (2 Timothy 3:16); and guides (Ephesians 4:13–14). But most of all it **leads us to Jesus Christ** (John 5:39) who is love (I John 4:8–9), the way, the truth, and the life (John 14:6).

Jesus promised that abiding in His Word leads to abundant living (John 10:10) and freedom (John 8:31–32, 36). Hopefully, you will find that studying the Bible will be a time that brings you great joy and delight. (Psalm 119:16,24).

Show me your ways, O LORD, teach me your paths;
guide me in your truth and teach me,
for you are God my Savior, and my hope is in you all day long.
Psalm 25:4–5

Your word is a lamp to my feet And a light to my path.
Psalm 119:105 NAS

All Scripture is God-breathed and is useful
for teaching, rebuking, correcting, and training in righteousness,
so that the man of God may be thoroughly equipped for every good work.
2 Timothy 3:16–17

So Jesus was saying..."If you continue in My word,
then you are truly disciples of Mine;
and you will know the truth, and the truth will make you free."
John 8:31–32 NAS

"Sanctify them by the truth; Your word is truth."
John 17:17

"I Have You in My Heart"

(1:7)

Philippians 1:1–11

Day 1
Background

1. From Acts 15:40–16:5, where and with whom did Paul minister before his trip to Philippi?

Digging Deeper
What do you learn about
Silas from Acts 15:22b,32 and
1 Peter 5:12?

   • Read Acts 16:7–10. Why did Paul and his fellow workers travel to Europe? (Macedonia was ancient Greece.)

FYI: "[Philippi] was located at the gateway between Europe and Asia and was like a miniature Rome, with a large number of Roman citizens. The Philippians were proud of their Roman heritage. They dressed like Romans and often spoke Latin. Many Philippians were retired military men who had been given land in the vicinity and who in turn served as a military presence there. Philippi was a wealthy town because of nearby gold and silver mines. Today the Greek city of Kavalla is located 9 miles from its ruins" (*NIV Archaeological Study Bible* 2005, 1925).

2. From Acts 16:11–12, how did Paul, Silas [Silvanus], Timothy, and Luke travel to Philippi? How is Philippi described? (The "we" in Acts 16:10 indicates that the author, Luke, joined them on the journey.)

3. Where and with whom did Paul and his team meet in Philippi (Acts 16:13)? What does this say about Paul, Silas, Timothy, and the gospel? See Galatians 3:28.

FYI: "Paul normally went first to a local synagogue when he arrived in a new city, but apparently there was none in Philippi. Since a group of only ten active men was required to constitute a synagogue, there must have been only a very small Jewish population there. The only such religious activity on the weekly Sabbath was apparently a ladies' prayer meeting, so that was where Paul headed. Despite this unpromising beginning, this gathering became the nucleus of the first Christian church in Europe" (Morris 1995, 1206).

4. List what you learn about Lydia from Acts 16:14.

    •   What actions did she take as a believer (16:15)? (See also 16:40.)

    > **FYI:** "Anyone who was a seller of purple dealt in a valued, luxurious product. The dyes used for making purple were expensive and highly regarded" (Guzik 2023).

5. How did a slave girl In Philippi bring her owners profit (16:16)?

6. What did the demon recognize (16:17)? How does that differ from a believing faith? (See James 2:19.)

7. How did Paul respond to the spirit (16:18)? What do you think grieved Paul?

8. Why were the owners upset (16:19)? Of what did they accuse Paul and Silas (16:20–21)?

    •   What does the city's response (Acts 16:22–24) say about the atmosphere and culture of Philippi?

9. From Acts 16:25 what witness did Paul and Silas give? What miracles did the Lord perform (16:26)?

    •   Who was added to the group of believers (16:27–33)?

10. Why do you think the magistrates decided to let Paul and Silas go (16:35)? Why did Paul refuse to leave (16:37)?

11. How were the magistrates affected by Paul's information (16:38–39)?

- Surprisingly, why don't you think Paul spared himself by claiming his Roman citizenship before the beating? (Contrast Acts 22:25–29.) What power would this have given Paul in preventing the magistrates in Philippi from coming after new believers?

ॐ **Applying the Word:** What are some principles you take away from Paul's example about evangelism and church planting?

ॐ

12. Read Chapter 1 of Philippians as if you were receiving this letter from Paul as your pastor and friend. How do you feel after reading it? What do you sense about his relationship with the readers and his major concerns for them?

> **Digging Deeper**
> As God's servant, what did Paul declare?
>
> – Titus 1:1
>
> – Ephesians 3:7, 8

13. Who sent the letter and to whom was it written (1:1)?

   • What does the title "servants" indicate about Paul's heart for the ministry?

> **FYI: servant/bondservant** "1401. *doulos;*...one who is in a permanent relation of servitude to another, his will being altogether consumed in the will of the other" (Zodhiates 1992, 483).

14. What change in obedience and service does a person have when they become a believer? See Romans 6:16–18.

15. In the following, mark (highlight, underline, circle...) the actions and attitudes that are involved in being a "servant" of Christ Jesus.

   • John 12:26 "Whoever serves me must follow me; and where I am, my servant also will be. My Father will honor the one who serves me."

   • Galatians 5:13 ...serve one another humbly in love.

   • 1 Peter 4:10 Each one should use whatever gift he has received to serve others, faithfully administering God's grace in its various forms.

16. How do we merit being called "saints/holy people" (1:1)? See 2 Timothy 1:9.

> **FYI: holy people/saints** "*hagios* (40)...In the plural, as used of believers, it designates all such and is not applied merely to persons of exceptional holiness...See 2 Thess. 1:10, where 'His saints' are also described as 'them that believed'" (Vine 1985, 544).

17. What does addressing bishops/overseers and deacons say about how this church (which began with two families) had developed and organized since Paul's first visit? (For the qualifications of a bishop/overseer/pastor and deacon, see 1 Timothy 3:1–13.)

- Read Ephesians 4:11–13. What was the purpose of people serving in these roles?

> **FYI:** "In the New Testament period, 'elder', 'pastor', and 'overseer' all represented one calling with the same responsibility to shepherd the flock" (Swindoll 2017, 35).

18. Why do you think "grace" comes before "peace" in Paul's greeting (1:2)? Compare Romans 5:1–2.

> **FYI:** Grace and peace to you "Paul's typical greeting throughout his letters (compare Gal. 1:3; Romans 1:7; Eph. 1:2; Philippians 1:2)" (Barry 2017, 1843).
>
> "This greeting could be called a summary of the gospel" (Evans 2019, 1405).
>
> "The two great heritages of the Christian are grace and peace. These are two things you can always have, no matter what your circumstances. Grace is all God's power, all his love, all his beauty available to you. It is a marvelous term which wraps up all that God is and offers to us... Peace is freedom from anxiety, fear, and worry.
>
> These are the two characteristics which ought to mark Christians all the time: Grace -- God at work in their life; and peace -- a sense of security, of trust" (Stedman 2024).

19. Who is the source of our peace (1:2)?

- From John 14:27 and 16:33, what did Jesus say about the peace He gives?

20. In the following, mark how we receive God's peace or the words that describe this peace.

- Isaiah 26:3 You will keep in perfect peace those whose minds are steadfast, because they trust in you.

- Philippians 4:6,7 Do not be anxious about anything, but in every situation, by prayer and petition, with thanksgiving, present your requests to God. [7] And the peace of God, which transcends all understanding, will guard your hearts and your minds in Christ Jesus.

- 2 Thessalonians 3:16 Now may the Lord of peace himself give you peace at all times and in every way. The Lord be with all of you.

- 2 Peter 1:2 Grace and peace be yours in abundance through the knowledge of God and of Jesus our Lord.

ദ **Applying the Word:** Who was instrumental in leading you to the Lord? If they were to write a letter to you, in what way(s) might they encourage you?

ദ

21. What characterized Paul's prayer for the Philippians (1:3)? Compare 1 Thessalonians 5:17–18.

- Why was Paul grateful for the Philippians (1:4–5)? Note "all" and "always" in 1:3–8.

> FYI: "**Partnership/fellowship** Strong's NT:2842 *koinonia* "A fellowship which is rooted in God and is a quest that can only be described as eternal" (Hughes 2007, 24).

22. How had the Philippians supported Paul and "participated/shown" a partnership with him.

- 1:5,7

- 1:19

- 1:30

- 2:25b

- 4:3

- 4:14–15

23. Underline other reasons for joy and gratitude about believers.

- Romans 1:8 First, I thank my God through Jesus Christ for all of you, because your faith is being reported all over the world.

- Romans 16:19 Everyone has heard about your obedience, so I am full of joy over you; but I want you to be wise about what is good, and innocent about what is evil.

- 1 Corinthians 1:4–6 I always thank God for you because of his grace given you in Christ Jesus. [5] For in him you have been enriched in every way—with all kinds of speech and with all knowledge—[6] God thus confirming our testimony about Christ among you.

- 1 Thessalonians 1:2–3 We always give thanks to God for all of you, making mention of you in our prayers; ³ constantly keeping in mind your work of faith and labor of love and perseverance of hope in our Lord Jesus Christ in the presence of our God and Father, NASB

- 1 Thessalonians 3:8–9 For now we really live, since you are standing firm in the Lord. ⁹ How can we thank God enough for you in return for all the joy we have in the presence of our God because of you?

- Ephesians 1:15–6 For this reason, ever since I heard about your faith in the Lord Jesus and your love for all God's people, ¹⁶ I have not stopped giving thanks for you, remembering you in my prayers.

- 3 John 1:3–4 It gave me great joy when some believers came and testified about your faithfulness to the truth, telling how you continue to walk in it. ⁴ I have no greater joy than to hear that my children are walking in the truth.

24. About what was Paul confident (1:6)? See also 1 Thessalonians 5:23–24. How encouraging do you think this would be?

> **FYI:** "It is neither our responsibility nor within our capability to maintain ourselves in a state of salvation. God began this work in us (Ephesians 2:8), and He will assure its continuance" (Morris 1995, 1315).
>
> **Video:** *Bible Project* "Overview of Philippians" https://bibleproject.com/explore/video/philippians/

25. In the following verses, underline other ways we can rely on God.

- 2 Thessalonians 1:11 With this in mind, we constantly pray for you, that our God may make you worthy of his calling, and that by his power he may bring to fruition your every desire for goodness and your every deed prompted by faith.

- 2 Corinthians 9:8 And God is able to make all grace abound to you, so that always having all sufficiency in everything, you may have an abundance for every good deed; NAS

- Hebrews 13:20–21 May the God of peace…²¹ equip you with everything good for doing his will, and may he work in us what is pleasing to him, through Jesus Christ, to whom be glory for ever and ever. Amen.

- 2 Peter 1:3 His divine power has given us everything we need for a godly life through our knowledge of him who called us by his own glory and goodness.

- Philippians 2:13 For it is God who works in you both to will and to do for His good pleasure. NKJ

- Philippians 4:13 I can do all things through Christ who strengthens me. NKJV

ঙ **Applying the Word:** What does partnering/fellowshipping in the gospel mean to you? With whom do you share your most meaningful fellowships?

ঙ

Day 4
Affection and Prayer. Read Philippians 1:7–11

26. How closely had the Philippian church's partnership with Paul bonded them together (1:7–8)? Write out the phrases Paul used to describe his affection for them.

- Why do you think Paul made an oath in 1:8 as he was saying this? (See also Romans 1:9, 2 Corinthians 11:31, and 1 Thessalonians 2:5.)

> **FYI:** "They were not...fair-weather Christians. When the gospel was spreading powerfully, they supported him. And when the name of Jesus landed Paul in a jail cell, the Philippian believers still remained true to him" (Evans 2019, 1405).

27. See examples of Paul's defense of the gospel in Acts 17:2–3, 18:4–5, and 19:8–10. What picture does this give you of his ministry? (Also see Paul's defense before King Agrippa in Acts 26:1–23.)

> **FYI: Defense of the gospel** (1:7,16) "'Defense' is the Greek *apologia*, a legal term referring to a formal defense as in a courtroom...The gospel was under attack in their day, and is even more so now, and it does need a sound defense...The apostle Peter enjoined us to be ready always to 'give an answer' (same Greek word, *apologia*), to anyone questioning why we believe the gospel (I Peter 3:15)" (Morris 1995, 1315).

28. By supporting and being identified with Paul's ministry and imprisonment, what were the Philippians risking? See Acts 17:5–6 and 19:29. Contrast 2 Timothy 4:16.

29. Summarize the emotions Paul displayed in:

- 1:3

- 1:4

- 1:6

- 1:7–8

> **Digging Deeper**
> Read Acts 15:36 and 18:23. What does this tell you about Paul's care for the churches he had founded?

Paul's prayer

30. What did Paul's affection for the Philippians cause him to seek for them (1:9a)? Compare 1 Thessalonians 3:12–13.

- In what ways was their love to grow (1:9b)? What does this say about the connection between love and knowledge?

- What difference do you see between knowledge and discernment/depth of insight?

> **FYI: knowledge** "1922. *epignosis;*...More intense than '*gnosis*' knowledge because it expresses a more thorough participation in the acquiring of knowledge on the part of the learner...a knowledge laying claim to personal involvement" (Zodhiates 1992, 624).
>
> "Love must be more than sentimental emotion; it must conform with the truth of the Word of God" (Evans 2019, 1405).

31. In the following list the contrasts made about love and knowledge.

- 1 Corinthians 13:1–3,8

- 1 Corinthians 8:1b

32. In the following, mark what is connected to knowledge.

- Ephesians 1:17 That the God of our Lord Jesus Christ, the Father of glory, may give you a spirit of wisdom and of revelation in the knowledge of Him.

- Ephesians 4:12–13 So that the body of Christ may be built up [13] until we all reach unity in the faith and in the knowledge of the Son of God and become mature, attaining to the whole measure of the fullness of Christ.

- Colossians 1:9 For this reason we also, since the day we heard about it, have not ceased praying for you and asking that you may be filled with the knowledge of His will in all spiritual wisdom and understanding, NAS

- Colossians 3:9–10 Do not lie to each other, since you have taken off your old self with its practices [10] and have put on the new self, which is being renewed in knowledge in the image of its Creator. NAS

- 1 Timothy 2:3–4 This is good, and pleases God our Savior, [4] who wants all people to be saved and to come to a knowledge of the truth.

- Luke 1:77 "To give his people the knowledge of salvation through the forgiveness of their sins."

- Habakkuk 2:14 For the earth will be filled with the knowledge of the glory of the LORD as the waters cover the sea.

33. How does 2 John 1:3, 6 connect love and truth?

- What does 1 Corinthians 13:6 say?

- From 1 John 4:7–8, who determines what love is?

> **FYI**: "Scripture teaches that love and truth are perfectly symbiotic. Try to separate truth from love or vice versa, and you destroy both virtues. Either virtue without its mate is merely a pretense. Love without truth has no character. Truth without love has no power. Love deprived of truth quickly deteriorates into sinful self-love. Truth divorced from love always breeds sanctimonious self-righteousness. Truth absent from love is harsh and heartless. Love from absent truth is hollow and hypocritical" (Johnson 2022).

34. To what would knowledge and discernment lead (1:10a)? See Romans 12:2b and Ephesians 4:22–23.

- According to Ephesians 4:14–15, what would this prevent?

> **FYI:** "The word translated '**discern**' is used to describe the process of testing coins so as to distinguish between those that are real and those that are counterfeit" (Coleman and Peace 1988, 19).

35. How would this love and knowledge be displayed?

- 1:10b

- 1:11a

36. Who is the source of our righteousness (1:11b)? Compare Philippians 3:9 and John 15:5.

- What "fruits of righteousness" does the Spirit produce in us (Galatians 5:22–23)?

> **FYI:** "Paul isn't telling the Philippians to let their love blind them to truth and righteousness so they end up overlooking sin and compromising holiness. That's a false interpretation of 'love' we often see in the world today. True Christian love is guided by the best interest of others. With true knowledge and discernment, love learns to spot the phony, the wrong, the evil. It learns to 'approve the things that are excellent' (1:10)" (Swindoll 2017, 38).

37. What is the ultimate goal of Christ's work in us (1:11c)? Cross-reference 2:11 and 4:20. (See John 15:8 and Matthew 5:16.)

- Compare Paul's prayer in Colossians 1:9–12 to his prayer in Philippians 1.

℘ **Applying the Word:** Try praying Paul's prayer in 1:9–11 for yourself or someone else.

Suggested Memory Verse:
"Being confident of this, that he who began a good work in you
will carry it on to completion until the day of Christ Jesus."
Philippians 1:6

Keywords in Chapter 1
Christ ☩
God
Spirit
joy (rejoice) ✧
gospel 📖
imprisonment (chains) ⛓
fellowship (participation, brothers, etc.) ♀♀♀

℘

"To Live is Christ"

(1:21)

Philippians 1:12–30

Day 1
Christi is Proclaimed. Read Philippians 1:12–18

1. Instead of writing about the hardships of prison, what perspective did Paul take (1:12)? What doubts about Paul and his ministry might the Philippian believers have had?

Digging Deeper
What other attitudes did Paul express about his imprisonment?

– 2 Timothy 2:9

– Ephesians 3:1,13

   • What verdict was handed down at Paul's trials (Acts 25:24–27 and 26:30–32)? How would that affect most people's attitudes?

2. How had Paul's imprisonment (chains) "advanced the gospel" (1:12)?

   • 1:13 (Compare 4:22)

   • 1:14

FYI: "Persons were imprisoned in Roman times while awaiting trial or execution, for political reasons or for ensuring compliance with a judicial order...Times of detention were neither limited nor strongly enforced, and ordinarily the prisoner was poorly treated. Many were beaten, tortured and given inadequate food and water, although a prisoner of higher status would often fare better.

While in Rome [Paul] was allowed to dwell outside the military camp, as well as to find and rent his own quarters. He received this relatively mild treatment for three reasons: [See Acts 28:30–31]

❖ Paul was a Roman citizen.

❖ He had received favorable verdicts from governors Festus and Agrippa.

❖ The Praetorian prefect overseeing prisoners from the provinces in the years A.D 51–62 was the honest Afranius Burrus.

Paul's trial took two years to conclude. According to Eusebius, Paul was released but later detained again in Rome when Nero began to execute Christians. Paul was at that point probably placed in the *tullianum*, the underground execution cell of the prison at Rome" (*NIV Archaeological Study Bible* 2005, 1826).

3. During his first confinement, what kind of an association did Paul have with the guards (Acts 28:16)? How would this compare to a jail?

- What had the Lord told Paul when he was arrested in Jerusalem (Acts 23:11)?

> FYI: "Palace guard...These men were the elite soldiers in the Roman army...Paul's guards were changed every four hours or so; thus he got the chance to witness to rotating coterie of soldiers from the key regiment in Rome" (Coleman and Peace 1988, 22).
>
> "As soldier after soldier was chained to him in successive watches, they heard the gospel both directly and from Paul's conversations with his visitors. My imagination hears the apostle's silent prayer as a new soldier is chained to him –'Thank you, Lord. Here's another one to tell about Jesus.' " (Hughes 2007, 48).

4. From the following verses, list the contrasts that describe the different motives and goals of those who preached Christ.

- 1:15

Digging Deeper
What does James 3:14–16 say about selfish ambition and envy? (See also Galatians 5:20)

- 1:16–17

- 1:18

> FYI: **add affliction to my chains** "Their competitive hearts didn't only want to win for themselves; they also wanted Paul to lose.
>
> They wanted Paul to admit the humiliation of having to admit that others were more effective in ministry than he was. They didn't understand that Paul honestly didn't care about this, because he did not have a competitive spirit in ministry" (Guzik 2023).

5. How did Paul react to the preaching of Christ no matter what (1:18)? How had he addressed them all in 1:14? What does that say about Paul's heart and motivation?

- How does this compare to Paul's reaction in Galatians 1:6–8 when false teachers distorted the truth of the gospel? Why do you think there is such a difference?

6. In 1 Thessalonians 2:2–8, what did Paul say his motives were or weren't in preaching the gospel?

 C3   **Applying the Word**: When has God used a difficulty in your life and turned it to good? When has a change in focus from yourself and your circumstances to Christ's love and presence in your life helped you see things differently?

C3

7. What is another reason that Paul rejoiced (1:19)? What two things did he depend on for his deliverance? Compare 2 Corinthians 1:10–11.

> **FYI: Deliverance/salvation** "G4991 *soteria*; rescue or safety (physically or morally):— deliver, health, salvation, save, saving" (Strong 2009, 1675).

8. Underline key parts of Paul's prayer requests in the following verses.

   - Romans 15:30–32 I urge you, brothers and sisters, by our Lord Jesus Christ and by the love of the Spirit, to join me in my struggle by praying to God for me. [31] Pray that I may be kept safe from the unbelievers in Judea and that the contribution I take to Jerusalem may be favorably received by the Lord's people there, [32] so that I may come to you with joy, by God's will, and in your company be refreshed.

   - Ephesians 6:19–20 Pray also for me, that whenever I speak, words may be given me so that I will fearlessly make known the mystery of the gospel, [20] for which I am an ambassador in chains. Pray that I may declare it fearlessly, as I should.

   - Colossians 4:2–4 Devote yourselves to prayer, being watchful and thankful. [3] And pray for us, too, that God may open a door for our message, so that we may proclaim the mystery of Christ, for which I am in chains. [4] Pray that I may proclaim it clearly, as I should.

   - 2 Thessalonians 3:1–2 As for other matters, brothers and sisters, pray for us that the message of the Lord may spread rapidly and be honored, just as it was with you. [2] And pray that we may be delivered from wicked and evil people, for not everyone has faith.

     ➢ What picture does this give you of Paul's dependence on and relationship with fellow believers in the ministry?

> **Digging Deeper**
> From 2 Corinthians 11:23–29, how difficult was Paul's ministry?

9. After rejoicing (1:18) and relying (1:19) on Christ, what did Paul "expect and hope" to do for Christ (1:20)? What do you think Paul meant by his death exalting Christ?

> **FYI: boldness/courage** "*parrhesia* (3954)...denotes (a), primarily, 'freedom of speech, unreservedness of utterance,'...(b) 'the absence of fear in speaking boldly; hence, confidence, cheerful courage, boldness'" (Vine 1985, 72).

> "Paul lived his life not to preserve and promote himself, but to glorify Jesus Christ. If Jesus should one day decide that Paul could best glorify Him through laying down his life, then Paul would be well pleased...Even so, this must have hit hard on the Philippians who saw God do so many remarkable miracles of deliverance in Paul's life among them in Philippi (Acts 16:11–40). It would have been easy for the Philippians to associate God's glory only with being delivered from one's problems, not in being delivered in the midst of one's problems" (Guzik 2023).

10. What associations did Paul make between life and death and Christ (1:21)? How would you state this in your own words? See Galatians 2:20.

- How did Paul say this in Romans 14:7–8?

> **FYI:** "Paul isn't saying that he wants to escape from life. He knows that his life, even in suffering, is filled with joy and fruitful labor...The 'now' is amazing because it's about serving Jesus, which brings meaning and joy. But he knows that the 'later' is better because it involves face-to-face communion with Christ (1 John 3:1–3)...You can't miss the Christ-centered passion of Paul It's all about Jesus—rejoicing in Jesus, relying on Jesus, and representing Jesus" (Merida and Chan 2016, 68).

11. Underline the wonders we can anticipate about eternal life.

- Job 19:26–27 "And after my skin has been destroyed, yet in my flesh I will see God; [27] I myself will see him with my own eyes—I, and not another. How my heart yearns within me!"

- Psalm 16:11 You have made known to me the path of life; you will fill me with joy in your presence, with eternal pleasures at your right hand.

- Isaiah 26:19 But your dead will live; their bodies will rise. You who dwell in the dust, wake up and shout for joy. Your dew is like the dew of the morning; the earth will give birth to her dead.

- 1 Corinthians 15:42–44 So will it be with the resurrection of the dead. The body that is sown is perishable, it is raised imperishable; [43] it is sown in dishonor, it is raised in glory; it is sown in weakness, it is raised in power; [44] it is sown a natural body, it is raised a spiritual body.

- Colossians 3:4 When Christ, who is your life, appears, then you also will appear with him in glory.

- 1 John 3:2 Dear friends, now we are children of God, and what we will be has not yet been made known. But we know that when Christ appears, we shall be like him, for we shall see him as he is.

- Jude 24 To him who is able to keep you from falling and to present you before his glorious presence without fault and with great joy.

- Revelation 21:3–4 And I heard a loud voice from the throne saying, "Now the dwelling of God is with men, and he will live with them. They will be his people, and God himself will be with them and be their God. ⁴ He will wipe every tear from their eyes. There will be no more death or mourning or crying or pain, for the old order of things has passed away."

12. How did Paul feel about the choice between life and death (1:22–23)?

13. From Acts 20:23–24, what did Paul know about the hardships he was facing? What focus did he take?

14. In the following verse, write out phrases describing the good purposes fulfilled if Paul continued to live.

- 1:22a e.g., *"fruitful labor for me"*

- 1:25

- 1:26

> **FYI:** "What a wonderful way to think about ministry: striving so that others may rejoice in all that is theirs in Christ" (Merida and Chan 2016, 71).
>
> "Paul was pleased to contribute to the spiritual growth of others so that their boasting in Christ Jesus [could] abound (1:26). But willingly laying down his life for the Philippians, Paul was simply following in the footsteps of his Master, Jesus Christ" (Evans 2019, 1405).

☙ **Applying the Word:** How would the belief that "to live is Christ" affect a person's relationships, time, attitudes, and actions?

☙

15. Although Paul did not know if or when he would be with the Philippians again, what concern did he have for them (1:27a)?

> **FYI: conduct/manner** (1:27) "G4176 *politeuomai;* to behave as a citizen (figuratively):— let conversation be, live" (Strong 2009, 1661).
>
> **worthy** (1:27) "G516 *axios*; appropriately" (Strong 2009, 1606).

16. Summarize how this worthy walk is described in:

   - Ephesians 4:1–3; 5:1–2

   - Colossians 1:10–12

17. Underline the titles that the Lord gives believers.

   - 2 Corinthians 5:20 We are therefore Christ's ambassadors, as though God were making his appeal through us. We implore you on Christ's behalf: Be reconciled to God.

   - Ephesians 2:19,22 Consequently, you are no longer foreigners and aliens, but fellow citizens with God's people and members of God's household...²² And in him you too are being built together to become a dwelling in which God lives by his Spirit.

   - Ephesians 5:1,8 Be imitators of God, therefore, as dearly loved children...⁸ For you were once darkness, but now you are light in the Lord. Live as children of light.

   - Colossians 3:12 Therefore, as God's chosen people, holy and dearly loved...

   - 1 Thessalonians 5:5 You are all sons of the light and sons of the day.

18. List the commands Paul gave for a worthy walk (1:27b–28a). How would each command keep them from succumbing to the world around them?

   - 1:27b

   - 1:27c

   - 1:28a (See Matthew 10:26–29)

19. Underline the results that unity in Christ produces.

- John 17:21, 23 "That all of them may be one, Father, just as you are in me and I am in you. May they also be in us so that the world may believe that you have sent me…²³ I in them and you in me. May they be brought to complete unity to let the world know that you sent me and have loved them even as you have loved me."

- Romans 15:5–6 May the God who gives endurance and encouragement give you a spirit of unity among yourselves as you follow Christ Jesus, ⁶ so that with one heart and mouth you may glorify the God and Father of our Lord Jesus Christ.

20. What conflicting messages does the gospel give people (1:28b)?

- How is this described in 2 Corinthians 2:15–16?

- In John 3:19–21, what reasons did Jesus give for these different reactions?

21. Mark destructive things that opponents/enemies of the gospel do.

- Romans 16:17 I urge you, brothers, to watch out for those who cause divisions and put obstacles in your way that are contrary to the teaching you have learned. Keep away from them.

- Galatians 1:6–7 I am astonished that you are so quickly deserting the one who called you by the grace of Christ and are turning to a different gospel— ⁷ which is really no gospel at all. Evidently some people are throwing you into confusion and are trying to pervert the gospel of Christ.

- 2 Peter 2:1–2 But there were also false prophets among the people, just as there will be false teachers among you. They will secretly introduce destructive heresies, even denying the sovereign Lord who bought them—bringing swift destruction on themselves. ² Many will follow their shameful ways and will bring the way of truth into disrepute.

- Jude 1:17–19 But, dear friends, remember what the apostles of our Lord Jesus Christ foretold. ¹⁸ They said to you, "In the last times there will be scoffers who will follow their own ungodly desires." ¹⁹ These are the men who divide you, who follow mere natural instincts and do not have the Spirit.

Ↄ   **Applying the Word:** What are the foundational truths you stand on without wavering? What are some examples of "nonessentials" that you would allow for differences of opinion?

Which do you feel is most challenging for a church: opposition from within or opposition from without? Why?

Ↄ

22. What two things have believers been called to do (1:29)? Compare Luke 9:23–25.

- How did the apostles react to suffering? See Acts 5:40–41.

> **FYI**: "The Philippians didn't need to fear that their present trial (and Paul's trial) meant that God had abandoned them. Their present difficulty was granted to them, not as a punishment, but as a tool in God's hand…If the Philippians had Paul's kind of conflict, they could also have Paul's kind of joy and fruit in the midst of it" (Guzik 2023).

23. From the following, mark what Christians were undergoing.

- 2 Corinthians 8:1–2 And now, brothers and sisters, we want you to know about the grace that God has given the Macedonian churches. ² In the midst of a very severe trial, their overflowing joy and their extreme poverty welled up in rich generosity.

- 1 Thessalonians 1:6–7 You became imitators of us and of the Lord, for you welcomed the message in the midst of severe suffering with the joy given by the Holy Spirit. ⁷ And so you became a model to all the believers in Macedonia and Achaia.

- Acts 8:1 …On that day a great persecution broke out against the church in Jerusalem, and all except the apostles were scattered throughout Judea and Samaria. NASB

24. Why is there suffering in this world?

- Romans 5:12

- 1 John 5:19

25. Why are believers often targeted for hatred and persecution? See John 15:18–25.

- In Matthew 10:16–22, what warning did Jesus give the disciples?

26. Underline how we should react to those who cause us suffering:

- Luke 6:27–28 "But I tell you who hear me: Love your enemies, do good to those who hate you, [28] bless those who curse you, pray for those who mistreat you."

- Romans 12:17–21 Do not repay anyone evil for evil. Be careful to do what is right in the eyes of everybody. [18] If it is possible, as far as it depends on you, live at peace with everyone. [19] Do not take revenge, my friends, but leave room for God's wrath, for it is written: "It is mine to avenge; I will repay," says the Lord....[21] Do not be overcome by evil, but overcome evil with good.

- 1 Peter 2:12 Live such good lives among the pagans that, though they accuse you of doing wrong, they may see your good deeds and glorify God on the day He visits us.

27. Underline what our perspective on suffering should be.

- Romans 8:18 I consider that our present sufferings are not worth comparing with the glory that will be revealed in us.

- 2 Corinthians 4:17–18 For our light and momentary troubles are achieving for us an eternal glory that far outweighs them all. [18] So we fix our eyes not on what is seen, but on what is unseen, since what is seen is temporary, but what is unseen is eternal.

- 2 Corinthians 12:9–10 But he said to me, "My grace is sufficient for you, for my power is made perfect in weakness." Therefore I will boast all the more gladly about my weaknesses, so that Christ's power may rest on me. [10] That is why, for Christ's sake, I delight in weaknesses, in insults, in hardships, in persecutions, in difficulties. For when I am weak, then I am strong.

28. Underline blessings that can come from suffering:

- Matthew 5:11–12 "Blessed are you when people insult you, persecute you and falsely say all kinds of evil against you because of me. [12] Rejoice and be glad, because great is your reward in heaven, for in the same way they persecuted the prophets who were before you."

- Romans 5:3–4 Not only so, but we also rejoice in our sufferings, because we know that suffering produces perseverance; [4] perseverance, character; and character, hope.

- 2 Corinthians 1: 5 For just as the sufferings of Christ flow over into our lives, so also through Christ our comfort overflows.

- 2 Corinthians 4:7 But we have this treasure in jars of clay to show that this all-surpassing power is from God and not from us.

- James 1:2–4 Consider it pure joy, my brothers and sisters, whenever you face trials of many kinds, [3] because you know that the testing of your faith produces perseverance. [4] Let perseverance finish its work so that you may be mature and complete, not lacking anything.

- 1 Peter 1:67 In all this you greatly rejoice, though now for a little while you may have had to suffer grief in all kinds of trials. [7] These have come so that the proven genuineness of your faith—of greater worth than gold, which perishes even though refined by fire—may result in praise, glory and honor when Jesus Christ is revealed.

- 1 Peter 4:13–14 But rejoice that you participate in the sufferings of Christ, so that you may be overjoyed when his glory is revealed. If you are insulted because of the name of Christ, you are blessed, for the Spirit of glory and of God rests on you.

29. How closely could the Philippians identify with Paul (1:30)? Compare 1 Thessalonians 3:3–4.

> **FYI:** "Paul's opposition came from secular merchants who were angry that he had freed a slave girl in bondage to an evil spirit. In Jerusalem, Paul's opposition came from religious Jews who saw his Christian faith as a threat to Judaism. The Philippians too, are facing this same sort of opposition. A group of Jewish proselytizers was advocating a return to the law with all its rules and regulations...In each instance Paul's struggle was with those who were opposed to his Christian beliefs and practices. In both cases his opponents stirred up the crowds against him and forced the Roman authorities to take him into custody. It is important to note that Paul was not being persecuted by Rome. His persecution originated with opponents of the gospel. The Philippians are also facing the same sort of opponents" (Coleman and Peace 1988, 30–31).

30. What picture does 1:27–30 give you of walking worthy of the gospel?

ℭ **Applying the Word:** In what ways have you been called to "contend/strive together" with other believers for the faith of the gospel? Have you ever been "alarmed/frightened" by opposition? What did you do?

Memory Verse:
"For to me, to live is Christ and to die is gain."
Philippians 1:21

ℭ

"Having the Same Love"

(2:2)

Philippians 2:1–11

Day 1
Serving One Another. Read Philippians 2:1–4

1. How would the qualities in 2:1 strengthen and unify believers?

   • "Encouragement/consolation in Christ" (See 2 Thessalonians 2:16–17.)

   • "Comfort of His love" (See 2 Corinthians 1:3.)

   • "Fellowship of the Spirit" (See Ephesians 2:18.)

   • "Tenderness/affection and compassion/mercy" (See Psalm 103:8–14.)

   > **FYI: Therefore** "This draws back to what Paul has built on in Philippians 1:27–30, telling the Philippians how to stand strong for the Lord against external conflicts. Now he tells them how to act against internal conflicts in the body of Christ...
   >
   > The word **consolation** (encouragement) in this passage is the ancient Greek word *paraklesis*. The idea behind this word for **consolation** in the New Testament is always more than soothing sympathy. It has the idea of strengthening, of helping, of making strong" (Guzik 2023).
   >
   > "The 'if' clauses imply a logical or reasonable relationship: Because these things are true, then there should be an attendant effect" (Swindoll 2017, 67).

2. From 2:2, list the effects that Christ's presence in our lives should have on attitudes and actions.

   • How would it make Paul feel if they walked in unity, humility, and unselfishness (2:2a)? See also Colossians 2:5 and 1 Thessalonians 3:7–9.

   > **FYI: mind** (2:2) "G5426 *phroneo*; to exercise the mind, i.e. entertain or have a sentiment or opinion; by implication, to be (mentally) disposed (more or less earnestly in a certain direction); intensively, to interest oneself in (with concern or obedience)" (Strong 2009, 1682).

3. Why is internal unity in the church so important? What difference do you see between unity and uniformity?

4. When we encounter disunity caused by error, deception, or a lack of understanding, how should we respond? See 2 Timothy 2:23–25.

5. List how we can accomplish and live out this unity (2:3–4). Note the word "but/rather" showing the contrasts.

   • What kind of community do you picture these behaviors creating?

6. In James 3:14–16, what are the origins and results of selfish ambition?

   > **FYI:** **"Selfish ambition** ...This is the second time Paul has used this word (see 1:17)...It means working to advance oneself without thought for others" (Coleman and Peace 1988, 23).
   >
   > **humility** "5012. *tapeinophrosune;*...Humility, lowliness of mind...For the sinner [it] involves the confession of his sin and a deep realization of his unworthiness to receive God's marvelous grace" (Zodhiates 1992, 1366).

7. If we consider someone above ourselves and they consider us above themselves, what happens to everyone's needs? What happens to any competitive spirit? What happens to the community?

   • Substitute the name of someone you are struggling with instead in the place of "others" in verses 2:3–4. How could you put that into practice?

8. In the following, underline attitudes or actions we should have.

   • Mark 9:35 Sitting down, Jesus called the Twelve and said, "If anyone wants to be first, he must be the very last, and the servant of all."

   • Romans 12:10 Be devoted to one another in brotherly love. Honor one another above yourselves.

   • Romans 12:16 Live in harmony with one another. Do not be proud, but be willing to associate with people of low position. Do not be conceited.

   • Romans 15:1–2 We who are strong ought to bear with the failings of the weak and not to please ourselves. ² Each of us should please his neighbor for his good, to build him up.

- Galatians 6:2 Carry each other's burdens, and in this way you will fulfill the law of Christ.

- 1 Peter 3:8 Finally, all of you, live in harmony with one another; be sympathetic, love as brothers, be compassionate and humble.

9. What did Jesus teach about honoring and serving others? See Matthew 20:25–28.

> **FYI:** "Christians are to accord others the same dignity and respect that Christ has given to all people. Humility involves seeing others not on the basis of how clever, attractive, or pious they are, but through the eyes of Christ who died for them" (Coleman and Peace 1988, 31).

10. In the following verses, underline the things associated with humility:

- Psalm 25:9 He guides the humble in what is right and teaches them his way.

- Proverbs 22:4 Humility is the fear of the LORD; its wages are riches and honor and life.

- Proverbs 11:2 When pride comes, then comes disgrace, but with humility comes wisdom.

- Prov. 29:23 A person's pride will bring him low, But a humble spirit will obtain honor. NASB

- James 4:6,10 That is why Scripture says: "God opposes the proud but shows favor to the humble."...10 Humble yourselves before the Lord, and he will lift you up.

- Luke 14:11 For all those who exalt themselves will be humbled, and those who humble themselves will be exalted.

- James 3:13 Who is wise and understanding among you? Let them show it by their good life, by deeds done in the humility that comes from wisdom.

11. From Galatians 6:14, what focus or understanding is needed for true humility?

ॐ **Applying the Word**: When has God called you to "look out for" someone's interests even when they interfered with your own? How did you lean on the Lord to work in and through you? What did you learn through that experience?

ॐ

Day 2
The Mind of Christ Jesus. Read Philippians 2:5–7

12. What attitude and mindset should we have (2:5)? See also Ephesians 5:1–2.

13. What do we need to understand first in order to appreciate Jesus's seven steps of humiliation in 2:7–8 (2:6)?

> **FYI: existed/being** (2:6) "Strong's NT:5225 *huparcho;* This is not the normal Greek word for 'being'…'It describes that which a man is in his very essence, that which cannot be changed' (Barclay). This word also carried the idea of pre-existence. By using it Paul is saying that Jesus always existed in the form of God" (Coleman and Peace 1988, 34).
>
> **robbery/something to be grasped** (2:7) "He was not fearful of losing His deity when He exchanged the outward form of God for the outward form of man…He could not cease being God" (Morris 1995, 1316).

14. What did John teach about Jesus's preincarnate existence in John 1:1–3,14; 3:13; 8:58, and 17:5?

15. Underline the divine titles/descriptions given to Jesus Christ in the following verses.

   • Isaiah 9:6 For to us a child is born, to us a son is given, and the government will be on his shoulders. And he will be called Wonderful Counselor, Mighty God, Everlasting Father, Prince of Peace.

   • Matthew 1:23 "Behold, the virgin shall be with child, and bear a Son, and they shall call His name Immanuel," which is translated, "God with us." NKJ

   • John 1:14 The Word became flesh and made his dwelling among us. We have seen his glory, the glory of the One and Only, who came from the Father, full of grace and truth. (See Gen. 1:1)

   • Colossians 1:15 He is the image of the invisible God, the firstborn of all creation. NASB

   • Colossians 2:9 For in Christ all the fullness of the Deity lives in bodily form,

   • Hebrews 1:3 The Son is the radiance of God's glory and the exact representation of his being, sustaining all things by his powerful word. After he had provided purification for sins, he sat down at the right hand of the Majesty in heaven.

- Revelation.1:7–8 "Look, he is coming with the clouds", and "every eye will see him, even those who pierced him"; and all the peoples of the earth "will mourn because of him." So shall it be! Amen. [8] "I am the Alpha and the Omega," says the Lord God, "who is, and who was, and who is to come, the Almighty."

16. Read Colossians 1:15–18. What authority does Jesus have?

17. What choice did Jesus make (2:7a)?

- Why did He do this (2 Corinthians 8:9)?

> **FYI: Emptied Himself /made Himself nothing** "2758. *keno;*...To empty oneself, to divest oneself of rightful dignity by descending to an inferior condition, to abase oneself" (Zodhiates 1992, 857).
>
> "He who once sat on the throne of the universe came to Earth 'lying in a manger' (Luke 2:12). Throughout His public ministry, He had 'no place to lay his head' (Matthew 8:20) Because He had no money to pay the tax, He had to catch a fish with the necessary coin in its mouth (Matthew 17:27). In His agony at Gethsemane, none of His friends would pray with Him, and when He was arrested they all 'forsook him and fled' (Matthew 26:40, 56). No one defended Him at His trial. On the cross, the soldiers stripped away His only personal possessions—the clothes on His back—and then 'parted his garments, casting lots upon them, what every man should take' (Mark 15:24). When He died, His body had to be buried in a tomb belonging to Joseph of Arimathea (Matthew 27:59-60). No home, no money, no possessions, no defenders, not even a tomb of His own in which to lie" (Morris July 2023).
>
> "In a state of absolute perfection and full control, Jesus willingly stepped out of His rightful realm of glory for the sake of humanity...When Philippians 2:7 says that Christ '**emptied Himself**,' it doesn't mean He gave up His deity or His divine attributes. It means He veiled them. In fact, He gave up the right to use them in situations in which He would have been entirely justified to use them, as He revealed in Matthew 26:53" (Swindoll 2017, 70).
>
> "Jesus added humanity; He didn't surrender deity...He surrendered His rights and prerogatives" (Merida and Chan 2016, 96–97).

18. What "form/nature" (*morphe*) did Jesus take upon Himself on earth (2:7b)? See Matthew 20:28.

19. In the following, what did Jesus teach about servanthood and how did He model it?

- Luke 22:24–27

- John 13:3–5

- Matthew 14:14

20. In Galatians 5:13–14, what command have we been given?

ↂ **Applying the Word:** When has someone's servant heart toward you been a powerful demonstration of God's love?

ↂ

Day 3
Christ's Humility and Death. Read Philippians 2:7–8

21. What was Jesus "made/born" as (2:7c)? See different translations. Compare Hebrews 10:5 and John 1:14.

> **FYI: likeness** (2:7) "G3667 *homoioma*; a form; abstractly, resemblance:— made like to, likeness, shape, similitude" (Strong 2009, 1653).
>
> "[Jesus] didn't empty Himself of deity; He didn't stop being God. Rather, He poured the fullness of deity into His humanity. He took on human flesh and became a servant...The incarnation resulted in Jesus being fully God and fully man" (Evans 2019, 1406).

22. How did Jesus appear to people on earth (2:8a)?

> **FYI: appearance/fashion** (2:8) "4976. *schema*;... the outward form...The eternal, infinite form of God took upon Himself flesh (John 1:1a; 14a)" (Zodhiates 1992, 997).
>
> "The opening phrase of 2:8 looks at [Christ] from the standpoint of how he **appeared** in the estimation of men. He was 'found' by them, as far as his external appearance was concerned as a mere man. Outwardly considered, he was no different from other men" (Gaebelein 1978, 124).

23. What did John say about Jesus's appearance in 1 John 1:1; John 1:14a?

24. How did people struggle with Jesus's identity?

   • Matthew 13:34–57

   • Luke 4:22

25. Underline the reasons why Jesus took on the form or appearance of a man.

   • Mark 10:45 "For even the Son of Man did not come to be served, but to serve, and to give his life as a ransom for many."

   • Luke 19:10 "For the Son of Man came to seek and to save what was lost."

   • John 6:38–40 "For I have come down from heaven not to do my will but to do the will of him who sent me. ³⁹ And this is the will of him who sent me that I shall lose none of all those he has given me, but raise them up at the last day. [40] For my Father's will is that everyone who looks to the Son and believes in him shall have eternal life, and I will raise them up at the last day."

- John 10:10 "The thief comes only to steal and kill and destroy; I have come that they may have life, and have it to the full."

- Romans 8:3 For what the law was powerless to do because it was weakened by the flesh, God did by sending his own Son in the likeness of sinful flesh to be a sin offering. And so he condemned sin in the flesh,

- Hebrews 2:14–15,17 Since the children have flesh and blood, he too shared in their humanity so that by his death he might destroy him who holds the power of death— that is, the devil—[15] and free those who all their lives were held in slavery by their fear of death... [17] For this reason he had to be made like them, fully human in every way, in order that he might become a merciful and faithful high priest in service to God, and that he might make atonement for the sins of the people.

- Hebrews 9:26 …But now he has appeared once for all at the end of the ages to do away with sin by the sacrifice of himself.

- 1 John 3:8 He who does what is sinful is of the devil, because the devil has been sinning from the beginning. The reason the Son of God appeared was to destroy the devil's work.

- 1 John 5:20 We know also that the Son of God has come and has given us understanding, so that we may know him who is true.

26. Underline the phrases describing Jesus's humanity.

- Luke 2:6–7 While they were there, the time came for the baby to be born, [7] and she gave birth to her firstborn, a son. She wrapped him in cloths and placed him in a manger, because there was no guest room available for them."

- Luke 2:52 And Jesus kept increasing in wisdom and stature, and in favor with God and people.

- John 4:6 Jacob's well was there, and Jesus, tired as he was from the journey, sat down by the well. It was about noon.

- Luke 22:44 And being in anguish, he prayed more earnestly, and his sweat was like drops of blood falling to the ground.

- Hebrews 4:15 For we do not have a high priest who is unable to empathize with our weaknesses, but we have one who has been tempted in every way, just as we are— yet he did not sin.

27. What does "obedience to death on the cross" (2:8b) say about the choice Christ had? Compare John 10:17–18.

28. What did death on a cross signify? See Deuteronomy 21:22–23 and Galatians 3:13.

- How did Jesus feel about dying on the cross? What motivated Him? See Hebrews 12:2 and Mark 14:36.

29. In the following, underline the extent Jesus's payment for sin.

- John 1:29 The next day John saw Jesus coming toward him and said, "Look, the Lamb of God, who <u>takes away the sin of the world</u>!"

- Colossians 2:13 When you were dead in your sins and in the uncircumcision of your flesh, God made you alive with Christ. He forgave us all our sins

- Hebrews 7:27 Unlike the other high priests, he does not need to offer sacrifices day after day, first for his own sins, and then for the sins of the people. He sacrificed for their sins once for all when he offered himself.

30. Mark why we need someone to die for us.

- Isaiah 53:6 We all, like sheep, have gone astray, each of us has turned to our own way; and the Lord has laid on him the iniquity of us all.

- Romans 3:10,23 As it is written: "There is no one righteous, not even one"...23 for all have sinned and fall short of the glory of God

- 1 Corinthians 15:50 I declare to you, brothers and sisters, that flesh and blood cannot inherit the kingdom of God, nor does the perishable inherit the imperishable.

31. From Ephesians 1:4a, when did Jesus determine to die and save us?

- According to (1 John 4:9–10), what did Christ's death demonstrate?

32. What have we been given because of Christ's payment on the cross? See John 1:12; 5:24.

    ℅   **Applying the Word:** How would you explain the "mindset" (2:5) that we are encouraged to have? How do you see this mindset (2:1–9) affecting relationships between friends, family, spouses, etc.? How should it affect those in positions of leadership?

℅

Day 4
Christ's Exaltation. Read Philippians 2:9–11

33. What was the "reason/therefore" (2:9) for Christ's exaltation?

   • What exaltation did Jesus receive (2:9b)?

   • How does Ephesians 1:20–23 describe this?

34. Who will bow their knee to Jesus Christ (2:10)?

   • In John 12:32, what did Jesus say He would accomplish by His death?

35. What final declaration will be made by all (2:11)? See Acts 2:36.

> **FYI**: "We also should not miss the significance that at a later time in the Roman Empire, all residents of the Empire were required to swear an oath of allegiance to the Emperor, declaring that Caesar is Lord, and burning a pinch of incense to an image of the emperor. Though the Roman state saw this only as a display of political allegiance, Christians rightly interpreted it as idolatry—and refused to participate, often paying with their lives" (Guzik 2023).

36. What does the name Lord (2:11) say about Jesus's authority? See Isaiah 42:8; 45:5a, 22–23.

   • What authority did Jesus claim in Matthew 28:18?

Just for Fun
Some believe that Philippians 2:5–11 was an early Christian hymn. If you were writing music for this passage, how would you like the different verses to be sung: loud, soft, slow, fast, major or minor key, instruments used, etc.?

> **FYI:** **Lord** "2962. *kurios*;... might, power, Lord, master, owner. Also the NT Greek equivalent for the OT Hebrews Jehovah" (Zodhiates 1992, 900).
>
> "**'Jesus'** (meaning 'the Lord saves') signifies that the Lord's salvation came when Jesus was born...**'Christ'** (meaning 'the Anointed,' 'the Messiah') speaks of His being the fulfillment of Old Testament prophecy...'**Lord**' is here understood to represent the divine name Yahweh which is a public declaration of His sovereignty" (Hughes 2007, 91,93).
>
> "His human name was Jesus ('Jehovah is Savior'), but this is used by itself only 22 times in the epistles—always with special emphasis on His humanity. Although it was the common name used repeatedly in the gospel narratives, it is significant that the disciples and other believers almost always addressed Him personally as Lord, never simply as Jesus. Unbelievers and demons, on the other hand, never addressed Him as Lord" (Morris Sept. 2023).

37. Mark what Christ's resurrection and exaltation means for us.

- John 16:7 "Nevertheless I tell you the truth; It is expedient for you that I go away: for if I go not away, the Comforter will not come unto you; but if I depart, I will send him unto you." KJV

- Romans 8:34 Who then is the one who condemns? No one. Christ Jesus who died—more than that, who was raised to life—is at the right hand of God and is also interceding for us.

- Ephesians 1:3 Blessed be the God and Father of our Lord Jesus Christ, who has blessed us with every spiritual blessing in the heavenly places in Christ, NASB

- Ephesians 2:6–7 And God raised us up with Christ and seated us with him in the heavenly realms in Christ Jesus, [7] in order that in the coming ages he might show the incomparable riches of his grace, expressed in his kindness to us in Christ Jesus.

- Colossians 3:1–4 Since, then, you have been raised with Christ, set your hearts on things above, where Christ is, seated at the right hand of God. [2] Set your minds on things above, not on earthly things. [3] For you died, and your life is now hidden with Christ in God. [4] When Christ, who is your life, appears, then you also will appear with him in glory.

38. Read through the following verses:

- John 5:22–23 "Moreover, the Father judges no one, but has entrusted all judgment to the Son, [23] that all may honor the Son just as they honor the Father. He who does not honor the Son does not honor the Father, who sent him."

- John 14:6 Jesus answered, "I am the way and the truth and the life. No one comes to the Father except through me."

- Acts 4:11–12 "Jesus is 'the stone you builders rejected, which has become the cornerstone.' [12] Salvation is found in no one else, for there is no other name under heaven given to mankind by which we must be saved."

- 1 Timothy 2:5–6. For there is one God and one mediator between God and mankind, the man Christ Jesus, [6] who gave himself as a ransom for all people...

- 1 John 2:23 No one who denies the Son has the Father; whoever acknowledges the Son has the Father also.

  ➢ How would you explain the way to God?

39. Although the way is narrow, mark the phrases that describe the broadness of the invitation and what it requires.

- John 3:16 For God so loved the world, that He gave His only Son, so that everyone <u>who believes in Him</u> will not perish, but have eternal life. NASB

- John 6:40 "For my Father's will is that everyone who looks to the Son and believes in him shall have eternal life, and I will raise them up at the last day."

- John 11:25–26 Jesus said to her, "I am the resurrection and the life; the one who believes in Me will live, even if he dies, [26] and everyone who lives and believes in Me will never die."

- John 10:7–9 So Jesus said to them again, "Truly, truly I say to you, I am the door of the sheep. [8] All those who came before Me are thieves and robbers, but the sheep did not listen to them. [9] I am the door; if anyone enters through Me, he will be saved, and will go in and out and find pasture." NASB

- Romans 10:12–13 For there is no difference between Jew and Gentile—the same Lord is Lord of all and richly blesses all who call on him, [13] for, "Everyone who calls on the name of the Lord will be saved." (Quoted from Joel 2:32. See Acts 2:21.)

40. Underline God's will concerning the salvation of people.

- 1 Timothy 2:3–4 This is good, and pleases God our Savior who wants all people to be saved and to come to a knowledge of the truth.

- Ezekiel 18:23 "Do I take any pleasure in the death of the wicked?" declares the Sovereign Lord. "Rather, am I not pleased when they turn from their ways and live?"

ଔ   **Applying the Word:** How does Christ's path of love and humility compare to the world's path of power? Which has the ability/power to truly transform lives from within?

Memory Verse:
"Do nothing out of selfish ambition or vain conceit.
Rather, in humility value others above yourselves,
not looking to your own interests but each of you to the interests of the others."
Philippians 2:3,4

Keywords in Chapter 2
Christ, God
joy (rejoice)
mind
work (toil, service)
but/rather

ଔ

"Shine as Lights in the World"

(2:15)

Philippians 2:12–30

Day 1
Work Out Your Salvation. Read Philippians 2:12–13

1. How does the "therefore/so then" in 2:12 connect with the preceding verses?

   • How did Paul commend the Philippians (2:12a)? What did he ask of them (2:12b)? Compare 1:27 and 1 Thessalonians 4:1,2.

2. What is the difference between working **out** (2:12) salvation but not working **for** salvation? (See 1:6.)

   • According to Ephesians 2:8,9, why can't we work for our salvation?

   > **FYI:** "We are not told to work for our salvation, but to work it out in practice in our lives. Our salvation is received entirely by grace through faith, not of works (Ephesians 2:8–9). Works can no more retain salvation for us than they can achieve it in the first place, but they are the visible evidence of salvation. We have been 'created' to do good works (Eph. 2:10)" (Morris 1995, 1317).

3. How do the attitudes described in Philippians 2:12b compare to Hebrews 12:28–29?

   • How do you feel that this kind of "fear" compares to the fear we experience in this world? See 1 John 4:18.

   > **FYI:** "**fear and trembling**...This phrase can refer to the sense of awe and wonder which a creature feels when standing before the creator. Such a sense of awe drives a person to seek and to do the will of God" (Coleman and Peace 1988, 38).

   > "To fear God is to take God seriously. We're to honor God in our decisions, regardless of the cost, so that He might be glorified. God brings circumstances into our lives, in fact, that will require us to 'work out' our salvation, to gain an increasingly high reverence for God and to choose His will over our own" (Evans 2019, 1407).

4. How are we empowered to work out our salvation (2:13a)?

- Why does God do this (2:13b)? What does this say about God's concern for your life and what you do with it? (See the use of the phrase His "pleasure" in Ephesians 1:5,9.)

> **FYI: Works** (2:13) "1754. *energeo;*...to effect, produce" (Zodhiates 1992, 589).
>
> **to will** (2:13) "G2309 *thelo* choose or prefer (literally or figuratively); by implication, to wish, i.e. be inclined to (sometimes adverbially, gladly)...by Hebraism, to delight in" (Strong 2009, 1633).

5. How did Paul describe the Lord's work in his life?

- Colossians 1:29

- 1 Corinthians 15:10

> **FYI:** "The Philippians are to work out their salvation not in the sense of earning it, but expressing the reality of their salvation through their practical obedience and selfless humility. The emphasis in on sanctification (learning to live more righteously), not on justification (being declared righteous)" (Swindoll 2017, 81).

6. How did Jesus describe God's work in our lives in John 15:1–5?

7. Mark ways that enable us to "work out" our salvation.

- Proverbs 3:5–6 Trust in the LORD with all your heart and lean not on your own understanding; in all your ways acknowledge him, and he will make your paths straight.

- Romans 12:2 Do not conform any longer to the pattern of this world, but be transformed by the renewing of your mind. Then you will be able to test and approve what God's will is–his good, pleasing and perfect will.

- 2 Corinthians 4:18 So we fix our eyes not on what is seen, but on what is unseen. For what is seen is temporary, but what is unseen is eternal.

- Galatians 5:25 If we live by the Spirit, let us also walk by the Spirit. NASB

- Ephesians 5:1–2 Follow God's example, therefore, as dearly loved children ² and walk in the way of love, just as Christ loved us and gave himself up for us as a fragrant offering and sacrifice to God.

- Ephesians 6:11 Put on the full armor of God so that you can take your stand against the devil's schemes.

- Hebrews 12:1 Therefore, since we are surrounded by such a great cloud of witnesses, let us throw off everything that hinders and the sin that so easily entangles, and let us run with perseverance the race marked out for us.

- 2 Peter 3:18 But grow in the grace and knowledge of our Lord and Savior Jesus Christ. To him be glory both now and forever! Amen.

- 2 Timothy 2:15 Do your best to present yourself to God as one approved, a workman who does not need to be ashamed and who correctly handles the word of truth.

ᘓ **Applying the Word:** Prayerfully read through Ephesians 3:16–21 concerning God's power available to us. Is there any way you doubt God's ability to work in you and give you the desire and the ability to accomplish His purposes? What do these verses indicate to you?

ᘓ

Day 2

Hold Firmly the Word of Life. Read Philippians 2:14–16

---

8. What did Paul warn against (2:14)? Why is this basic to a community standing strong in the face of opposition?

    • How all-encompassing was this command? Why is it tempting to grumble? What focus can keep us from grumbling? See Hebrews 12:2,3.

> **FYI: grumbling/arguing** "*gongusmos* (1112); a murmuring, muttering...is used of...displeasure or complaining" (Vine 1985, 422).
>
> **disputing/arguing** "G1261 *dialogismos;* discussion, i.e. (internal) consideration...or (external) debate" (Strong 2009, 1617).

9. When traveling through the wilderness, how had the Israelites failed to trust the Lord? See Exodus 15:22–24;16:2–3 and Numbers 13:31–4:4

> **Digging Deeper**
> See Nehemiah 9:9–15, 19–21 for a list of the miraculous protection and blessings the Israelites were given.

10. In Deuteronomy 1:31; 2:7 and 29:5, what do you learn about how carefully the Lord had led the nation out of Egypt and provided for them?

    • Despite this, how had they responded (Numbers 14:22)?

11. Although God loved the nation, what did their grumbling prevent God from giving them? See Numbers 14:23, 29–31.

    • What did grumbling say about their hearts and their trust in God? What did it do to their ability to receive God's mercy and blessings? See Jude 21.

> **FYI:** "Biblical data is clear that we can take ourselves out of the place where God can righteously express his love toward us...Complaining shows a serious distrust in God's goodness and sovereignty...Even the best covenant relationships can be hindered or cultivated by the faithfulness or lack of it by the parties involved" (Miller 2023, Numbers video).

12. What does the command in 2:14, along with the ones in 2:3–4, suggest about problems Philippian believers were having?

13. How do 1 Corinthians 3:3 and James 4:1–3 describe the mindset behind disputes?

Digging Deeper
In the following verses, why did people grumble about Jesus?

– Luke 15:2; 19:7

– Mark 14:4–5

– John 6:41–43

   • Contrast David's prayer in Psalm 139:23–24.

14. Underline the consequences of complaining and disputing.

   – Corinthians 1:10 I appeal to you, brothers, in the name of our Lord Jesus Christ, that all of you agree with one another so that there may be no divisions among you and that you may be perfectly united in mind and thought.

   – Galatians 5:15 If you keep on biting and devouring each other, watch out or you will be destroyed by each other.

   – Proverbs 26:20–21 Without wood a fire goes out; without a gossip a quarrel dies down. 21 As charcoal to embers and as wood to fire so is a quarrelsome person for kindling strife.

   – Proverbs 15:1 A gentle answer turns away wrath, but a harsh word stirs up anger.

15. See the behaviors in 1 Corinthians 10:6–10 that we are told not to do. What does this say about the seriousness of murmuring?

   • With what other behaviors did Jude link grumbling in Jude 1:16?

16. When we keep from grumbling and arguing, what witness do we give (2:15)?

> **FYI: Crooked/warped** "G4646 *skolios*; warped, i.e. winding; figuratively, perverse" (Strong 2009, 1669).
>
> **Perverse/crooked** "G1294 *diastrepho*; to distort, i.e. (figuratively) misinterpret, or (morally) corrupt" (Strong 2009, 1618).

17. Read through the following verses describing the things that should characterize our speech and behavior. Mark things that are meaningful to you.

- Romans 14:19 So then we pursue the things which make for peace and the building up of one another. NASB

- Romans 15:1–2 We who are strong ought to bear with the failings of the weak and not to please ourselves. ² Each of us should please our neighbors for their good, to build them up.

- 1 Corinthians 16:14 Let all that you do be done with love. NKJV

- Ephesians 4 29–32 Do not let any unwholesome talk come out of your mouths, but only what is helpful for building others up according to their needs, that it may benefit those who listen. ³⁰ And do not grieve the Holy Spirit of God, with whom you were sealed for the day of redemption. ³¹ Get rid of all bitterness, rage and anger, brawling and slander, along with every form of malice. ³² Be kind and compassionate to one another, forgiving each other, just as in Christ God forgave you.

- Colossians 3:8–10 But now you must also rid yourselves of all such things as these: anger, rage, malice, slander, and filthy language from your lips. ⁹ Do not lie to each other, since you have taken off your old self with its practices ¹⁰ and have put on the new self, which is being renewed in knowledge in the image of its Creator.

- Colossians 4:6 Let your conversation be always full of grace, seasoned with salt, so that you may know how to answer everyone.

- James 1:19–20 My dear brothers and sisters, take note of this: Everyone should be quick to listen, slow to speak and slow to become angry, ²⁰ because man's anger does not produce the righteousness that God desires.

- 1 Peter 3:15–16 Always be prepared to give an answer to everyone who asks you to give the reason for the hope that you have. But do this with gentleness and respect, ¹⁶ keeping a clear conscience, so that those who speak maliciously against your good behavior in Christ may be ashamed of their slander.

18. What will help us maintain this witness to the world (2:16a)? Do you think the commands in 2:14 and 2:16a relate to each other?

- Who and what is the "Word of life"? See 1 John 1:1–3 and John 6:63b,68.

> **FYI: holding fast/hold out** "G1907 *epecho;* to hold upon, i.e. (by implication) to retain...to pay attention to:— give (take) heed unto, hold forth, mark, stay" (Strong 2009, 1627).
>
> "**holding fast** could also be translated holding forth. Both meanings are true and Paul could have meant it in this dual sense" (Guzik 2023).
>
> "The Scriptures constitute 'the word of life' in written form. Jesus Christ is 'the Word of life' in human form (I John 1:1)" (Morris 1995, 1317).

19. In John 9:5 what did Jesus say about Himself? What did He say about believers? See Matthew 5:13–16.

20. Mark the descriptions of being a light and what that light can do.

   • Daniel 12:3 Those who are wise will shine like the brightness of the heavens, and those who lead many to righteousness, like the stars for ever and ever.

   • Proverbs 4:18 The path of the righteous is like the morning sun, shining ever brighter till the full light of day.

   • Ephesians 5:8–13 For you were once darkness, but now you are light in the Lord. Live as children of light ⁹ (for the fruit of the light consists in all goodness, righteousness and truth) ¹⁰ and find out what pleases the Lord. ¹¹ Have nothing to do with the fruitless deeds of darkness, but rather expose them. ¹² For it is shameful even to mention what the disobedient do in secret. ¹³ But everything exposed by the light becomes visible— and everything that is illuminated becomes a light.

21. How troubled was Paul by the thought that the Philippians might be straying from the truth (2:16b)? Compare 1 Thessalonians 3:5.

22. Mark what we are to "hold unto" or "remain in."

   • John 8:31–32 To the Jews who had believed him, Jesus said, "If you hold to my teaching, you are really my disciples. ³² Then you will know the truth, and the truth will set you free."

   • John 15:4 "Remain in me, and I will remain in you. No branch can bear fruit by itself; it must remain in the vine. Neither can you bear fruit unless you remain in me."

   • Acts 11:23 When he arrived and saw the evidence of the grace of God, he was glad and encouraged them all to remain true to the Lord with all their hearts.

   • 1 Corinthians 15:2 By this gospel you are saved, if you hold firmly to the word I preached to you

- 1 Timothy 3:9 They must keep hold of the deep truths of the faith with a clear conscience.

- 1 Timothy 6:12 Fight the good fight of the faith. Take hold of the eternal life to which you were called when you made your good confession in the presence of many witnesses.

- Titus 1:9 He must hold firmly to the trustworthy message as it has been taught, so that he can encourage others by sound doctrine and refute those who oppose it.

- Hebrews 4:14 Therefore, since we have a great high priest who has gone through the heavens, Jesus the Son of God, let us hold firmly to the faith we profess.

- Hebrews 10:23 Let us hold unswervingly to the hope we profess, for he who promised is faithful.

℞ **Applying the Word:** What are some good ways to respond when you encounter grumbling and complaining? Can you think of ways to break any habitual grumblings or murmurings you engage in?

℞

Day 3
Timothy. Read Philippians 2:17–23

23. What attitude did Paul have about his trials (2:17)? Compare 1:17–18.

- How did Paul want the Philippians to respond to them (2:18)?

> **FYI: drink offering/libation** "A priest would offer a sacrifice and then later pour out a sacrificial libation to complement it...[Paul} viewed his service as a complement or contribution to their service" (Hughes 2007, 101).

24. What did Paul say in:

- 2 Corinthians 12:15a

- Acts 20:24

- 1 Thessalonians 2:8

25. How did Paul want to use Timothy's service (2:19) and why? What does this say about Paul's heart for believers?

26. What made Timothy so special to Paul (2:20)? Compare 2:4.

> **FYI: Like-minded** "2473. *isopsuchos*;...To be activated by the same motives, of like character, like-minded" (Zodhiates 1992, 783).

27. What was motivating some people (2:21)? Contrast Paul's goals in 1:21a and 2:17.

28. How did Paul regard Timothy's work in the ministry (2:22)? See also 1 Corinthians 16:10.

29. In Acts 16:1–4, what do you learn about how Timothy came into the ministry? (Acts 14:8–23 gives the account of Paul's missionary work in Lystra where Timothy may have first heard him.)

30. What do Paul's descriptions in 2:20–22 indicate to you about Timothy?

    • "Like-minded/kindred spirit"

    • "genuine concern/sincerely care"

    • "proven worth/character"

    • "as a son with his father he served"

31. Mark other phrases Paul used to describe Timothy and the ministry he had been given.

    • 1 Thessalonians 3:2–3 We sent Timothy, who is our brother and co-worker in God's service in spreading the gospel of Christ, to strengthen and encourage you in your faith, so that no one would be unsettled by these trials...

    • 1 Corinthians 4:17 For this reason I have sent to you Timothy, my son whom I love, who is faithful in the Lord. He will remind you of my way of life in Christ Jesus, which agrees with what I teach everywhere in every church.

    • 1 Timothy 1:2 To Timothy my true son in the faith...

    • 2 Timothy 1:2 To Timothy, my beloved son... NASB

32. From 2 Timothy 1:5–6; 3:10–11, 15, list the training and experience Timothy had.

> **Digging Deeper**
> What are some other places where Timothy ministered?
>
> Acts 19:22
>
> 1 Timothy 1:3

33. Near the end of Paul's life, what are some instructions about ministry that he gave Timothy?

    • 1 Timothy 1:3–4 *refute false doctrines and teachings*

    • 1 Timothy 4:13–16

    • 2 Timothy 1:13–14

- 2 Timothy 2:1–3

- 2 Timothy 2:14–16

- 2 Timothy 4:2,5

34. How would you summarize Paul's relationship with Timothy and the hopes he had for him?

> **FYI:** "**Timothy**: When the apostle was a prisoner at Rome, Timothy joined him (Phil 1:1), where it appears he also suffered imprisonment (Heb 13:23). During the apostle's second imprisonment he wrote to Timothy, asking him to rejoin him as soon as possible, and to bring with him certain things which he had left at Troas, his cloak and parchments (2 Tim 4:13).
>
> According to **tradition**, after the apostle's death he settled in Ephesus as his sphere of labour, and there found a martyr's grave" (Easton 2024).

35. When did Paul want to send Timothy to Philippi (2:23)?

- What expectation did Paul have (2:24)? Cross-reference 1:19.

☙ **Applying the Word:** Do you have people in your life who are "like-minded" in their beliefs, and who love and serve Christ? How would you describe what these people mean to you? How do they encourage and help you?

☙

Day 4
Epaphroditus. Read Philippians 2:24–30

36. Record the titles Paul gave to Epaphroditus in 2:25. What do these communicate about him?

37. How had Epaphroditus served the Philippians and Paul (2:25b; 4:18)?

> **FYI:** "Epaphroditus served in no public capacity...All he did was faithfully discharge his duty by delivering a bag of money to Paul and then by looking after him. We must understand that to serve in some unnoticed, unrecognized place in the body of Christ is as much the work of Christ as is public ministry" (Hughes 2007, 115).

38. What do the concerns Epaphroditus had for his friends and family back home say about his character (2:26)?

39. How sick had Epaphroditus been (2:27a)?

- How did Paul feel about Epaphroditus's recovery (2:27b)? How does that compare to his concern for himself (1:21–24)?

40. What other reasons did Paul give for sending Epaphroditus back to Philippi (2:28)?

- Why might the Philippians have heard about Epaphroditus's illness but not his recovery? (Note: To ensure safety and provide accountability, there would have been a group of men with Epaphroditus carrying the gift to Paul. See 2 Corinthians 8:18–22.)

41. How did Paul want the Philippians to receive Epaphroditus (2:29)?

- How highly did Paul praise him (2:30)?

42. How was Epaphroditus's attitude like Paul's (2:17)?

> **FYI: Risking/not regarding his life** "In the present context it means Epaphroditus was willing to die. In those days when you visited prisoners held by the Romans, the visitor was often prejudged as a criminal also. Therefore the visitor exposed himself to danger just by being near those who were considered dangerous. This word came to also be used in the sense of playing the gambler or playing dice because high sums were often at stake. In a sense Epaphroditus was gambling with his life for the sake of God's kingdom" (Garland 2024).

☞ **Applying the Word:** Think of someone to encourage by letting them know a positive attribute/ strength/gift that you see in them.

Memory Verses:
"For it is God who works in you to will and to act
in order to fulfill his good purpose."
Philippians 2:13

"Do everything without grumbling or arguing,
so that you may become blameless and pure,
'children of God without fault in a warped and crooked generation.'
Then you will shine among them like stars in the sky
as you hold firmly to the word of life…"
Philippians 2:14–16

℘

"Rejoice in the Lord"

(3:1)

Philippians 3:1–11

Day 1
Rejoice in the Lord. Read Philippians 3:1–3

1. Despite circumstances, where can we find joy (3:1)? (Compare "rejoice/take pride in Christ Jesus" in 3:3.) How do you think rejoicing serves as a "safeguard"?

> **FYI: Rejoice** "G5463 *chairo*; to be 'cheerful', i.e. calmly happy or well-off; impersonally, especially as salutation (on meeting or parting), be well" (Strong 2009, 1683).
>
> **Safe/safeguard** "804. *asphales*;...Firm, that which cannot be thrown down...sure, steady, immovable (Heb. 6:19 of an anchor)...safe, secure from peril" (Zodhiates 1992, 283).

2. What did Nehemiah say about joy in Neh. 8:10b? See also Habakkuk 3:18–19.

3. List the terms Paul used to describe the people causing trouble (3:2). What does the threefold repetition of the word "beware" indicate?

> **FYI:** "During the time of the early church many devout Jews were willing to accept Jesus as Messiah, but they wanted to hold on to forms of Judaism. They believed that Gentiles had to become Jews before becoming Christians. This involved the act of circumcision and taking on the law of Moses (Carson)" (Merida and Chan 2016, 134).
>
> "The exact identity of these opponents is impossible to pin down...But they may have been... the Judaizers about whom Paul wrote in Galatians...They are really the **evil-doers** because they rely for their righteousness on their own good works instead of God's grace." (Coleman and Peace 1988, 46).
>
> **"Dogs** were coyote-like scavengers who fed on roadkill, carrion, filth, and garbage—they were vivid images of the unclean" (Hughes 2007, 123).

4. From the beginning what problem had arisen among Jewish and Gentile believers (Acts 15:1,5)? What did Peter conclude in Acts 15:10–11?

5. Read Genesis 17:3–14. What did circumcision represent (17:11)? Why would being uncircumcised seem wrong or profane to many Jewish people (17:14)?

> **FYI: Circumcision** "A ritual cutting away of the foreskin, signifying that a man is a Jew...The cutting represented an oath that invoked a curse on oneself; it invited God to cut off the man's life and heirs if he broke his covenant with God. Circumcision also demonstrated that a life (the sex organ represented life) was being set apart for God. Paul liked to quote Moses' and Jeremiah's teaching that true circumcision is 'circumcision of the heart'—that is, obedience in faith (Romans 2:28–29; compare Deuteronomy 10:16; Jeremiah 4:4)" (Lee-Thorp 1987, 74).

6. From the letter to the Galatians, what did Paul say believers were doing when they brought circumcision in as a requirement for salvation rather than trusting in Christ's work?

   • Galatians 5:2

   • 5:3

   • 5:4a

   • 5:4b

7. What motives did false teachers have, and how did Paul react in Galatians 2:4–5?

   • How strongly did he condemn this teaching in Galatians 1:8–9?

8. Paul became uncharacteristically harsh in Phil. 3:2. What was at stake? Contrast Paul's instruction for dealing with sin issues in Galatians 6:1.

   ☙ **Applying the Word:** How do you think you can practice rejoicing in the Lord even amid sorrow, anxiety, depression, fear, disappointment, anger, etc...?

   How is repeating the gospel an expression of love for both believers and unbelievers?

☙

9. What three qualities define genuine believers who are "the true circumcision" (3:3)?

> **FYI:** "To say that we must worship God 'in spirit' means, among other things, that it must originate from within, from the heart; it must be sincere, motivated by our love for God and gratitude for all he is and has done. Worship cannot be mechanical or formalistic. That does not necessarily rule out certain rituals or liturgy. But it does demand that all physical postures or symbolic actions must be infused with heartfelt commitment and faith and love and zeal" (Storms 2020).

10. Record how Paul defined "true circumcision" (3:3) in:

   • Romans 2:28–29

   • Colossians 2:11

> **Digging Deeper**
> Which came first in Abraham's life: faith or circumcision? See Romans 4:1–3. Why is that important (4:9–14)?

11. How is worship/serving God defined in Romans 12:1? (How do Romans 12:2 and 6:12–13 describe the process?)

12. Mark what the Spirit of God gives us or does for us.

   • John 14:26 "But the Advocate, the Holy Spirit, whom the Father will send in my name, will teach you all things and will remind you of everything I have said to you."

   • Ephesians 1:17 I keep asking that the God of our Lord Jesus Christ, the glorious Father, may give you the Spirit of wisdom and revelation, so that you may know him better.

   • 1 Corinthians 2:12 What we have received is not the spirit of the world, but the Spirit who is from God, so that we may understand what God has freely given us.

   • John 16:13–14 "But when he, the Spirit of truth, comes, he will guide you into all the truth. He will not speak on his own; he will speak only what he hears, and he will tell you what is yet to come. [14] He will glorify me because it is from me that he will receive what he will make known to you."

- Romans 8:1–2, 26–27 Therefore, there is now no condemnation for those who are in Christ Jesus, ² because through Christ Jesus the law of the Spirit who gives life has set you free from the law of sin and death... ²⁶ the Spirit helps us in our weakness. We do not know what we ought to pray for, but the Spirit himself intercedes for us through wordless groans. ²⁷ And he who searches our hearts knows the mind of the Spirit, because the Spirit intercedes for God's people in accordance with the will of God.

- Galatians 5:16, 22–23 So I say, walk by the Spirit, and you will not gratify the desires of the flesh...²² But the fruit of the Spirit is love, joy, peace, forbearance, kindness, goodness, faithfulness, ²³ gentleness and self-control. Against such things there is no law.

- 2 Timothy 1:7 For God has not given us a spirit of timidity, but of power and love and discipline. NASB

13. How does following the Spirit compare to following the law? See 2 Corinthians 3:6 and John 6:63.

14. According to Romans 7:18 and 8:3, what made the law ineffective?

15. In whom do we boast/glory/rejoice (3:3c)? See 1 Corinthians 1:30–31 and Jeremiah 9:24.

- From Romans 3:27–28, why is there no room for boasting in ourselves? Compare Ephesians 2:8–9.

> **FYI: boast/rejoice in Christ Jesus** (3:3) "We boast because it is not our hold on Christ that saves us—it is Christ. We boast because it is not our joy in Christ that saves us—it is Christ. We boast because it is not even our faith that saves us—it is Christ...Christ becomes the singular concern and focus of His people" (Hughes 2007, 125).

16. In what shouldn't we put our confidence (3:3d)?

- From Galatians 6:15, how much value does circumcision have?

> **FYI:** "Christ followers 'put no confidence in the flesh.' They rejoice in the Lord—not in human works, not in personal piety, not in anything but the person and work of Christ" (Swindoll 2017, 104).

17. When people reverted to trying to earn salvation by works, of what did Paul remind them in Galatians 3:1–4?

Digging Deeper
What was Jesus's answer to the question about what to **do** to inherit eternal life (John 6:28–29)? See also John 5:38–40

• Why can't works be a part of grace (Romans 11:6)?

18. What new way did Christ give us (Romans 7:4–6)?

ᘓ **Applying the Word:** Do you feel comforted or unsettled by the command that you should "put no confidence in the flesh"? In what things other than Christ are you tempted to put your confidence? How does the command to put no confidence in the flesh free you and change your focus?

ᘓ

Day 3
Count as Loss. Read Philippians 3:4–11

19. If human accomplishments were what we could boast about, how did Paul measure up (3:4)?

> **FYI: flesh** "G4561 *sarx*; flesh...i.e. (strictly) the meat of an animal (as food), or (by extension) the body (as opposed to the soul [or spirit], or as the symbol of what is external...or (by implication) human nature (with its frailties [physically or morally] and passions), or (specifically) a human being (as such):— carnal, carnally minded...fleshly" (Strong 2009, 1668).
>
> "Paul anticipates the response of these Jewish enemies to what he has just said about the lack of value of law and ritual. He knows they will claim that he says all this because he is a Christian and not an authentic Jew. To answer this charge Paul lays out before them his rather substantial credentials as a Jew (verses 4–6)" (Coleman and Peace 1988, 47).

20. List the lineage, training, and achievements that Paul could have confidence in from a fleshly (worldly) viewpoint (3:5,6).

> **Digging Deeper**
> For historical people that brought fame to the tribe of Benjamin, see:
> 1 Samuel 9:1–2;
> 2 Samuel 19:14–18;
> 1 Kings 12:21

> **FYI:** "Paul is no proselyte, circumcised in later life as some of his enemies might have been... Paul was a true-blooded Jew from the cradle, and nursed in the ancestral faith. Therefore he speaks with an authority which none can challenge, least of all the opponents whose main tenet...may have been the need of circumcision. Paul would counter this false notion by placing circumcision at the head of the list to show that he has the right to be heard on the true significance of the rite...In regard to his devotion to the law...he could own his membership of the strictest sect of his religion (Acts 26:5), the Pharisees (Galatians 1:14)" (Martin 1995, 145–146).
>
> "Paul was in every way the match of his opponents in Philippi. He had lived at the very pinnacle of Judaism" (Coleman and Peace 1988, 47).
>
> "Notice that Paul didn't say he was sinless or perfect but '**blameless**.' The Pharisees assumed that a faithful Israelite could keep the Torah's 613 commandments because the Law provided rituals and procedures to receive forgiveness and purifications" (Hughes 2007, 131).

21. What did Paul say about God's forgiveness and mercy toward him, in spite of his persecution of the church (1 Timothy 1:12–16)?

Digging Deeper
What do you learn about Paul's religious zeal and accomplishments from:

Galatians 1:14

Acts 22:4–5; 26:9–11

22. Why did the zeal of many Jewish people become a barrier to faith (Romans 10:1–3)?

23. Note the word "loss" in 3:7–8 What did Paul count/ consider as loss and why? What did he want to know or gain instead?

FYI: loss "G2209 *zemia*; detriment" (Strong 2009, 1632).

"The Greek term used for **'loss'**...is also used in Acts 27:10 for the cargo and lives lost in a shipwreck" (Swindoll 2017, 108).

Gain "*kerdaino* (2770),...metaphorically, to win persons...or so practically appropriating Christ to oneself that He becomes the dominating power in and over one's whole being and circumstances, Phil 3:8" (Vine 1985, 260).

Rubbish "4657. *skubalon*;...That which is thrown to the dogs, dregs, refuse, what is thrown away as worthless. Spoken of the refuse of grain, chaff, or of a table, of slaughtered animals, of dung, and figuratively of the filth of the mind" (Zodhiates 1992, 1298).

"'**Excellency/surpassing worth'** means 'higher authority.' That is, the knowledge of Christ as Savior and Lord is higher than all the secular and religious knowledge Paul had learned in his scholastic training as a Pharisee. Similarly, it is higher than any knowledge one could ever acquire from modern science or philosophy, or from any other discipline" (Morris 1995, 1318).

---

24. Consider where Paul was and what he had gone through as an apostle for Christ. In what kinds of "things" could Paul have boasted? See 2 Corinthians 11:21–29. Instead, what did Paul say he would boast about (2 Cor. 11:30)?

Digging Deeper
How did Paul describe his weaknesses in 1 Corinthians 2:3–5?

25. Underline the things that we know through Christ Jesus.

• John 1:17 For the law was given through Moses; grace and truth came through Jesus Christ.

• John 14:6–7 Jesus answered, "I am the way and the truth and the life. No one comes to the Father except through me.[7] If you really knew me, you would know my Father as well. From now on, you do know him and have seen him."

- 2 Corinthians 4:6 For God, who said, "Let light shine out of darkness," made his light shine in our hearts to give us the light of the knowledge of the glory of God in the face of Christ.

- 2 Peter 1:2 Grace and peace be yours in abundance through the knowledge of God and of Jesus our Lord.

- 1 John 3:16 This is how we know what love is: Jesus Christ laid down his life for us.

- 1 John 5:13 I write these things to you who believe in the name of the Son of God so that you may know that you have eternal life.

- 2 Timothy 1:12 ...for I know whom I have believed and am persuaded that He is able to keep what I have committed to Him until that Day. NKJV

- Romans 8:28 And we know that in all things God works for the good of those who love him, who have been called according to his purpose.

26. Underline what we have when we "gain/win" in Christ.

- Romans 5:1 Therefore, since we have been justified through faith, we have peace with God through our Lord Jesus Christ,

- Romans 8:1 Therefore, there is now no condemnation for those who are in Christ Jesus,

- 2 Corinthians 5:17 Therefore, if anyone *is* in Christ, *he is* a new creation; old things have passed away; behold, all things have become new. NKJ

- John 5:24 "Truly, truly, I say to you, the one who hears My word, and believes Him who sent Me, has eternal life, and does not come into judgment, but has passed out of death into life." NASB

- Ephesians 1:3–4 Blessed *be* the God and Father of our Lord Jesus Christ, who has blessed us with every spiritual blessing in the heavenly *places* in Christ, [4] just as He chose us in Him before the foundation of the world, that we should be holy and without blame before Him in love." NKJV

- Galatians 2:20a I have been crucified with Christ and I no longer live, but Christ lives in me.

- Colossians 1:22 But now he has reconciled you by Christ's physical body through death to present you holy in his sight, without blemish and free from accusation.

- Titus 3:7 So that, having been justified by his grace, we might become heirs having the hope of eternal life.

27. Think of someone you have a close relationship with that makes you feel like you know and understand them. What did it take to have that kind of relationship? How does this apply to your relationship with Christ and **knowing** Him?

ଔ **Applying the Word:** Read through Paul's prayers for believers in Ephesians 1:17–23 and 3:14–21 as if Paul was praying them over you. How does this affect your perspective of who you are?

Which request for understanding do you desire to be fulfilled in your heart and mind?

ଔ

Day 4
Be Found in Him. Read Philippians 3:9–11

28. Why did Paul want to be found in Christ (3:9)? What two types of "righteousness" are contrasted in 3:9b? How is righteousness obtained?

> **FYI**: "To keep the law...the Creator Himself had to become man, and...fulfill the law as our representative before God. Then, when He died, Christ 'redeemed us from the curse of the law, being made a curse for us' (Galatians 3:13). 'But now apart from the law the righteousness of God has been made known...through faith in Jesus Christ to all who believe.' (Romans 3:21–22)" (Morris 1996).

29. Why can't we achieve righteousness on our own? Galatians 3:10–12

   • Why is righteousness by faith superior to the law (Romans 8:3–5)?

30. What happens if we do everything right except for one thing (James 2:10)?

> **FYI**: "Here's the problem. Only righteous people are going to heaven. Yet none of us are righteous (Rom. 3:9–18). Therefore, we need another source of righteousness, and that's why the gospel is good news. As Paul says here in Philippians 3 and elsewhere, believers have received the righteousness that comes from God through faith in Christ alone...What a glorious exchange! Christ received our punishment though He never sinned, and we received His righteousness though we didn't deserve it. Consequently we are found in Christ. This means that God sees us through the righteousness of Christ. Believers are now protected from judgment, and we can know that we have forgiveness from God and are accepted by God. No better news exists.
>
> How infinitely different Christianity is from other religions. In other systems, you have to do the work. In Christianity, Christ did the work We rejoice in those wonderful words, 'It is finished!' " (Merida and Chan 2016, 141–142).

31. List the ways that Paul wanted to "know" Christ in his life (3:10).

> **FYI:** "The word for **know** here [3:10] is the same form used in 3:8, referring to a personal experiential knowledge. To know Christ is more than merely to know facts or doctrine about him. Paul wanted to know Christ better and better, for Christ had changed the very foundation of his life. That should be the goal of every believer—to know Christ more fully and personally, and that can be a lifelong process" (Barton 1995, 95).

32. What does Christ's resurrection power (3:10) mean for us?

- Romans 8:11,34

- Colossians 1:11

33. Underline reasons that believers fellowship in Christ's sufferings (3:10).

- John 15:18–20 "If the world hates you, keep in mind that it hated me first. [19] If you belonged to the world, it would love you as its own. As it is, you do not belong to the world, but I have chosen you out of the world. That is why the world hates you. [20] Remember what I told you: 'A servant is not greater than his master.' If they persecuted me, they will persecute you also."

- Ephesians 6:10–12 Finally, be strong in the Lord and in his mighty power. [11] Put on the full armor of God, so that you can take your stand against the devil's schemes. [12] For our struggle is not against flesh and blood, but against the rulers, against the authorities, against the powers of this dark world and against the spiritual forces of evil in the heavenly realms.

34. Why was Christ willing to suffer (John 10:11)?

- According to Isaiah 53:4–8, what did He do for us?

35. In Matthew 27:12–14, what responses did Christ have to suffering and abuse? See also 1 Peter 2:23 and Isaiah 53:7.

- What could Jesus have done at any time (Matthew 26:52–56)?

36. From the following, list the phrases describing the reasons Paul gave for suffering for Christ.

- 2 Corinthians 4:7–11

- 2 Timothy 2:9–10

- Colossians 1:24

37. In the following, underline the promises and assurances that are given about suffering.

- Matthew 5:11–12 "Blessed are you when people insult you, persecute you and falsely say all kinds of evil against you because of me. [12] Rejoice and be glad, because great is your reward in heaven, for in the same way they persecuted the prophets who were before you."

- 1 Corinthians 10:13 No temptation has seized you except what is common to man. And God is faithful; he will not let you be tempted beyond what you can bear. But when you are tempted, he will also provide a way out so that you can stand up under it.

- 2 Corinthians 1:3–5 Praise be to the God and Father of our Lord Jesus Christ, the Father of compassion and the God of all comfort, [4] who comforts us in all our troubles, so that we can comfort those in any trouble with the comfort we ourselves have received from God. [5] For just as the sufferings of Christ flow over into our lives, so also through Christ our comfort overflows.

- James 1:2–4 Consider it pure joy, my brothers and sisters, whenever you face trials of many kinds, [3] because you know that the testing of your faith produces perseverance. [4] Let perseverance finish its work so that you may be mature and complete, not lacking anything.

- 1 Peter 1:6–7 In this you greatly rejoice, though now for a little while you may have had to suffer grief in all kinds of trials. [7] These have come so that your faith—of greater worth than gold, which perishes even though refined by fire—may be proved genuine and may result in praise, glory and honor when Jesus Christ is revealed.

- 1 Peter 4:13–14 But rejoice inasmuch as you participate in the sufferings of Christ, so that you may be overjoyed when his glory is revealed. [14] If you are insulted because of the name of Christ, you are blessed, for the Spirit of glory and of God rests on you.

38. What was Paul anticipating (3:11)? Compare 2 Timothy 1:12.

FYI: Resurrection "Strong's NT:1815 *exanastasis* (from ek = out of or from + anistemi = to rise up) refers to the state or condition of coming up from among the dead. Literally it is the 'out resurrection' a graphic word used only here in the NT" (Garland 2024).

There are different ways of interpreting Philippians 3:11, such as:

"The resurrection was certain, but the intervening events were uncertain as to timing and circumstances" (Hughes 2007, 142).

"This resurrection may very well refer to the one experienced by those resurrected first from among all the dead (1 Cor. 15:23 ['every man in his own order']; 1 Thess. 4:16; Rev. 20:5)" (Zodhiates 1992, 599).

"[Paul] is talking about experiencing Jesus's resurrection power in this life to joyously overcome every challenge" (Evans 2019, 1408).

ℭ **Applying the Word:** It has been said that, "Whatever you do to **get love** you will ultimately resent. But whatever you do as a **response to love** you will never regret." Where do you see your works as an effort to try to earn God's love? How do you think things could be different if you always saw yourself as perfectly loved and responded to it?

Memory Verse:
"And be found in Him,
not having a righteousness of my own that comes from the law,
but that which is through faith in Christ—
the righteousness that comes from God on the basis of faith."
Philippians 3:9

Keywords in Chapter 3
rejoice
Lord (Christ)
God
flesh
righteousness
count/consider
loss
mind
live/walk

ℭ

"Forgetting What is Behind"

(3:13)

Philippians 3:12–21

Day 1
Pressing On. Read Philippians 3:12–14

1. What did Paul say about his progress in walking with the Lord (3:12a)? How does this compare to his attitude in the past (3:6b)?

> **FYI: perfect** "G5048 *teleioo*; to complete, i.e. (literally) accomplish, or (figuratively) consummate (in character):— consecrate, finish, fulfill, (make) perfect" (Strong 2009, 1676).
>
> **press on** "1377. *dioko;* to follow or press hard after, to pursue with earnestness and diligence in order to obtain, to go after with the desire of obtaining" (Zodhiates 1992, 474).
>
> "The reality is, the more we come to know Christ, the more we will come to sense our need to grow" (Hughes 2007, 146).
>
> "Paul was on the same path as every one of us. He had been justified (declared righteous by God) on the basis of the merits of Christ, and like all of us, he was in the process of being sanctified as he looked forward to one day being glorified through resurrection. Perfection in this life is not possible. We are frail, fallen, feeble humans; and we will continue in this state until our death" (Swindoll 2017, 116).

2. Toward whose goal was Paul "pressing on" (3:12b)? What do you think he meant?

   • For what reason had the Lord "taken hold/apprehended" Paul? See Acts 9:15; 26:16–18.

3. Mark what we continually need to be doing.

   • 2 Peter 1:5–7 For this very reason, make every effort to supplement your faith with goodness, goodness with knowledge, ⁶ knowledge with self-control, self-control with endurance, endurance with godliness, ⁷ godliness with brotherly affection, and brotherly affection with love.

   • 2 Peter 3:18 But grow in the grace and knowledge of our Lord and Savior Jesus Christ. To him be the glory both now and to the day of eternity.

   • Romans 12:2 Do not be conformed to this age, but be transformed by the renewing of your mind, so that you may discern what is the good, pleasing, and perfect will of God.

- Colossians 1:9–10 ...We continually ask God to fill you with the knowledge of his will through all the wisdom and understanding that the Spirit gives, ¹⁰ so that you may live a life worthy of the Lord and please him in every way: bearing fruit in every good work, growing in the knowledge of God.

- Philippians 2:12 Therefore, my dear friends, as you have always obeyed—not only in my presence, but now much more in my absence—continue to work out your salvation with fear and trembling.

- Ephesians 2:8,10 for you were once darkness, but now you are light in the Lord; walk as children of light ...¹⁰ as you try to learn what is pleasing to the Lord. NASB

4. Record the verb phrases in 3:13b that describe the attitude Paul had about his past and future.

    - How can looking back at successes or failures keep us from moving forward (2 Peter 1:9)?

    - From 1 Timothy 1:13,15, what are some failures Paul (Saul) needed to forget to "press on"?

5. What was Paul's goal (3:14)?

6. Besides a "high" calling, mark how our calling is described, or what it is connected with, in the following verses.

    - 1 Corinthians 1:9 God is faithful, who has called you into fellowship with his Son, Jesus Christ our Lord.

    - Romans 1:6 And you also are among those Gentiles who are called to belong to Jesus Christ.

- Romans 1:7 To all in Rome who are loved by God and called to be his holy people...

- Eph. 1:18 I pray that the eyes of your heart may be enlightened in order that you may know the hope to which he has called you, the riches of his glorious inheritance in his holy people,

- 2 Timothy 1:9 He has saved us and called us to a holy life....

Digging Deeper
What does scripture say about rewards/prizes?

– 1 Corinthians 3:12–15; 4:5

– Matthew 16:27

– James 1:12

– 2 Timothy 4:8

- Hebrews 3:1 Therefore, holy brothers and sisters, who share in the heavenly calling...

- 1 Peter 2:9 ...that you may declare the praises of him who called you out of darkness into his wonderful light.

- 1 Peter 5:10 And the God of all grace, who called you to his eternal glory in Christ...

7. In the following, underline goals for believers:

- Romans 8:29 For those God foreknew he also predestined to be conformed to the image of his Son, that he might be the firstborn among many brothers and sisters.

- Colossians 1:28 We proclaim Him, admonishing every person and teaching every person with all wisdom, so that we may present every person complete in Christ. NASB

- 2 Thessalonians 1:11–12 With this in mind, we constantly pray for you, that our God may make you worthy of his calling, and that by his power he may bring to fruition your every desire for goodness and your every deed prompted by faith. [12] We pray this so that the name of our Lord Jesus may be glorified in you, and you in him, according to the grace of our God and the Lord Jesus Christ.

8. Paul often compared striving for the "prize" to a race. What advice did he give about running?

- 1 Corinthians 9:24–27

- Hebrews 12:1–3

9. In another analogy (1 Tim. 1:18–19), what advice did Paul give about fighting "the good fight"?

ߐ **Applying the Word:** What does this passage in Philippians indicate about God's view of our proud self-achievements or humiliating failures in the past? What do you need to forget as you "run the race"?

ߐ

10. What "attitude/way of thinking" was Paul referring to in 3:15a?

- What was Paul confident God would do (3:15b)? See James 1:4–5.

> **FYI:** "Apparently, in the Philippian church, there were those who tended to think differently, i.e. to adopt a different viewpoint from that given in Paul's teaching and to act upon it...There may have been a group in the Philippian church who professed a spiritual attainment superior to that of the rest of their fellow-believers...So confident is he that the truth has been stated, that he invokes the aid of God to illuminate the minds and correct the behavior of those who do not share his conviction (cf. Gal 5:10)" (Martin 1995, 158).

11. To what standard should be living (3:16)? See 1 John 2:3–5.

- In Mark 4:24–25, what did Jesus say about responsibility toward what we know or have?

> **FYI:** "Paul would not allow a lack of understanding to excuse anyone from doing what he *did* know to be the Lord's will. What we *don't know* can never excuse us from failing to fulfill what we *do know* to do" (Guzik 2023)
>
> "No one...must wait for God to reveal the truth on all points before he begins to give himself to spiritual growth. Each believer should exercise fully the degree of maturity he already possesses. 'Live up to'...calls for Christians to maintain a consistent life in harmony with the understanding of God's truth they already have. Paul recognizes that Christians, though proceeding along the same path, may be at different stages of progress and should be faithful to as much of God's truth as they understand" (Gaebelein 1978, 143).

12. Whose examples did Paul encourage believers to follow (3:17)? See Hebrews 13:7.

- Whose example did Paul point to in Ephesians 5:1–2?

- Why could Paul encourage them to follow his example (3:17)? See I Corinthians 11:1.

13. List the phrases in 3:18–19 describing people who were not walking in truth. How strongly did Paul feel about this apostasy?

> **FYI:** "These '**enemies of the cross**' were probably Judaizers—those Jewish Christians who were overly zealous for their law. But some scholars think Paul was referring to another false teaching that had surfaced, called 'antinomianism.' Those who subscribed to this teaching believed that once their souls had been redeemed by Christ, what they did in their bodies no longer mattered. Thus they threw aside morality and decency, believing that nothing done in the body could stain their already-redeemed souls" (Barton 1995, 104).
>
> **Their god is their belly** "It was not merely the pleasures of the stomach that was their god, but the bodily desires and sensual delights that displaced the divine and became their god" (Hughes 2007, 157).
>
> "[Judaizers] were obsessed with laws relating to what they could eat and drink, how and when to eat, ritual preparation for eating, etc. A key feature of their religious life thus involved the issue of food... food laws and circumcision had become gods to these people (Hawthorne)" (Coleman and Peace 1988, 51).

14. Underline the words describing false **teachers** and the characteristics of their **teaching**:

- Matthew 7:15–16a "Beware of the false prophets, who come to you in sheep's clothing, but inwardly are ravenous wolves. [16] You will know them by their fruits...." NASB

- Romans 16:17–18 I urge you, brothers and sisters, to watch out for those who cause divisions and put obstacles in your way that are contrary to the teaching you have learned. Keep away from them. [18] For such people are not serving our Lord Christ, but their own appetites. By smooth talk and flattery they deceive the minds of naive people.

- 2 Corinthians 11:13–15 For such people are false apostles, deceitful workers, masquerading as apostles of Christ. [14] And no wonder, for Satan himself masquerades as an angel of light. [15] It is not surprising, then, if his servants also masquerade as servants of righteousness.

- Colossians 2:4 I tell you this so that no one may deceive you by fine-sounding arguments.

- I Timothy 1:3–7 command certain people not to teach false doctrines any longer [4] or to devote themselves to myths and endless genealogies. Such things promote controversial speculations rather than advancing God's work—which is by faith. [5] The goal of this command is love, which comes from a pure heart and a good conscience and a sincere faith. [6] Some have departed from these and have turned to meaningless talk.

- 1 Timothy 6:4–5 ...They have an unhealthy interest in controversies and quarrels about words that result in envy, strife, malicious talk, evil suspicions [5] and constant friction between people of corrupt mind, who have been robbed of the truth and who think that godliness is a means to financial gain.

- Hebrews 13:9 Do not be carried away by varied and strange teachings. NAS

- 2 Peter 2:1–3 But there were also false prophets among the people, just as there will be false teachers among you. They will secretly introduce destructive heresies, even denying the sovereign Lord who bought them—bringing swift destruction on themselves. [2] Many will follow their shameful ways and will bring the way of truth into disrepute. [3] In their greed these teachers will exploit you with stories they have made up...

- Jude 1:4 For certain individuals whose condemnation was written about long ago have secretly slipped in among you. They are ungodly people, who pervert the grace of our God into a license for immorality and deny Jesus Christ our only Sovereign and Lord.

15. In contrast to the "enemies of Christ", where should a believer's focus be (3:20)?

- What do we need to guard against (Colossians 2:8)?

> **Digging Deeper**
> See the nature of some erroneous teachings.
>
> – Acts 15:1,5
>
> – I Timothy 4:1–3
>
> – 2 Peter 3:3–6
>
> – Colossians 2:16–17

- How does knowing scripture (2 Timothy 3:16–17) protect us?

16. How would you describe the opposites of the four descriptions in 3:19?

- "Destruction" vs. salvation and eternal life

- "Appetite" vs.

- "Glory is in their shame" vs.

- "Earthy" things vs.

17. In 1 Thessalonians 2:1–12, how did Paul describe and contrast his care of the churches?

CB **Applying the Word:** What do Paul's commands say to you about the privilege, responsibility, and challenges of being a witness for Christ?

CB

> **FYI:** 'Who were these '**enemies of the cross of Christ'?** [3:18] Some regard them as the Judaizers of 3:2, whose emphasis on legalism undermined the effect of the Cross...Others view them as antinomians, who went to the opposite extreme from the Judaizers and threw off all restraints... By their lawless lives, they too were enemies of the Cross and the new life that should issue from it" (Gaebelein 1978, 147).

18. In Acts 20:29–31, what did Paul say would eventually happen to the gospel?

Lawlessness (Antinomianism/License)

19. How did some people reason incorrectly and misuse their freedom found in Christ (Romans 6:1,15)?

   • Why is living without any standards or showing restraint (license) a form of slavery (Romans 6:16–17)?

20. How did Paul deal with licentiousness in the Corinthian church (1 Corinthians 5:1–5)? Why were they "proud"? Why was tolerating this sin not showing love?

> **FYI:** "The word antinomianism comes from two Greek words, *anti*, meaning 'against'; and *nomos*, meaning 'law.' Antinomianism means 'against the law.' Theologically, antinomianism is the belief that there are no moral laws God expects Christians to obey. Antinomianism takes a biblical teaching to an unbiblical conclusion. The biblical teaching is that Christians are not required to observe the Old Testament Law as a means of salvation. When Jesus Christ died on the cross, He fulfilled the Old Testament Law (Romans 10:4; Galatians 3:23–25; Ephesians 2:15). The unbiblical conclusion is that there is no moral law God expects Christians to obey" (Got Questions 2007).
>
> "In its more extreme and perverted form, antinomianism permits immoral behavior based on the leniency of grace" (Ligonier 2023).

21. According to 1 John 2:3–6, what does disobedience to God's commands say about our belief in Jesus Christ?

22. In the following verses, underline the response believers should have to licentiousness and immorality.

- 1 Corinthians 6:18 Flee from sexual immorality....

- Ephesians 4:22 You were taught, with regard to your former way of life, to put off your old self, which is being corrupted by its deceitful desires.

- Ephesians 5:3 But among you there must not be even a hint of sexual immorality, or of any kind of impurity, or of greed, because these are improper for God's holy people.

- 1 Thessalonians 5:21–22 but test everything; hold fast what is good, [22] abstain from every form of evil. RSV

- 1 Peter 2:11–12 Dear friends, I urge you, as aliens and strangers in the world, to abstain from sinful desires, which war against your soul. [12] Live such good lives among the pagans that, though they accuse you of doing wrong, they may see your good deeds and glorify God on the day he visits us.

- Galatians 5:13 You, my brothers and sisters, were called to be free. But do not use your freedom to indulge the flesh; rather, serve one another humbly in love.

Legalism

23. Why can **legalism** look appealing or sound good?

- Luke 16:15; 18:9

- Matthew 23:27–28

> FYI: "**Legalism** is the insistence that a person is accepted by God on the basis of his law keeping. It teaches that we are declared righteous before God through our own observance of either God's law or man-made rules and regulations....The inclination to earn salvation is rooted in our sin nature. **Legalism** feeds on the sinful pride of mankind by offering a way to make up for the wrongs we have done. Legalism convinces the consciences of people that they have in themselves what they need to attain righteousness before God and men" (Ligonier 2023).

24. To what attitude do works often lead (Ephesians 2:9)?

- What is the appeal (Genesis 3:5)?

25. From Galatians:

- How does a legalistic attitude affect Christ's work on the cross (Galatians 2:21)?

- What motivated legalists (6:12–13)?

- What does legalism do to our relationship with God (5:4a)?

> **Digging Deeper**
> See Paul's comments about legalistic rules in Colossians 2:16–17, 20–23.

- How did Paul feel about legalism (4:9–11)?

- What response did he say believers should have to legalism (5:1)?

26. According to Romans 4:14, what does depending on works for salvation say about faith?

The Place of Works

27. Although we are not saved by works, why should we do good works? See Ephesians 2:10; 4:1.

28. What instructions are given about works in:

- Romans 6:13

- Galatians 5:16–18

> **FYI:** "We aren't righteous on our own. We aren't even good. It's only through the blood of Christ that God can look at us as though we lived Christ's perfect life. When we put legalistic requirements on ourselves and others, we remove the power and necessity of Christ. We elevate ourselves, dangerously assuming we have the capacity to please God on our own.
>
> God wants our hearts first, because a heart that loves Him will naturally produce works that glorify Him...He wants us to love Him so that He can produce righteousness in us. Without Christ, any 'good' thing we produce will be utterly worthless. *'Abide in Me, and I in you. As the branch cannot bear fruit of itself unless it abides in the vine, so neither can you unless you abide in Me.' (John 15:4)*" (Burns 2019).

29. Mark the reasons/blessings for living a life of obedience and Christ-likeness.

- Matthew 7:24–25 "Therefore everyone who hears these words of mine and puts them into practice is like a wise man who built his house on the rock. [25] The rain came down, the streams rose, and the winds blew and beat against that house; yet it did not fall, because it had its foundation on the rock."

- 1 Timothy 4:8 For physical training is of some value, but godliness has value for all things, holding promise for both the present life and the life to come.

- 1 Timothy 6:18–19 Command them to do good, to be rich in good deeds, and to be generous and willing to share. [19] In this way they will lay up treasure for themselves as a firm foundation for the coming age, so that they may take hold of the life that is truly life.

- James 1:25 But the man who looks intently into the perfect law that gives freedom, and continues to do this, not forgetting what he has heard, but doing it—he will be blessed in what he does.

- 2 Peter 1:4 Through these he has given us his very great and precious promises, so that through them you may participate in the divine nature and escape the corruption in the world caused by evil desires.

30. From 2 Corinthians 5:14–15, what should motivate us?

> **FYI:** "The message of Christ crucified cures legalism and antinomianism. As we recognize that Jesus died to atone for our lawlessness (1 John 3:4), we will desire to live a life of obedience to His commandments. When we understand that Christ is the source of sanctification for believers (1 Cor. 1:30), we long to be conformed more and more to His image" (Ligonier 2023).

☙ **Applying the Word:** Sin has been defined as "missing the mark" (of God's best for our lives) or as "self-defeating behavior." How do you see both legalism and licentiousness fitting those descriptions?

☙

31. Compare Philippians 3:20a with Ephesians 2:5–6, 19.

   • What mindset should that give us? Colossians 3:1–2ff

32. As citizens of heaven, underline the identity or responsibility we have.

   • 1 Corinthians 3:9 For we are co-workers in God's service; you are God's field, God's building.

   • 1 Corinthians 3:16 Do you not know that you are a temple of God and *that* the Spirit of God dwells in you? NASB

   • 2 Corinthians 5:20 Therefore, we are ambassadors for Christ, as though God were making an appeal through us; we beg you on behalf of Christ, be reconciled to God. NASB

   • Ephesians 2:22 And in him you too are being built together to become a dwelling in which God lives by his Spirit.

33. What hope do we have (3:20b)?

   • As a citizen of heaven awaiting a heavenly Savior, how should these first-century believers in Philippi have viewed their Roman citizenship and allegiance to Caesar who was called a savior and a god?

   FYI: "Saviour, *sōtēr*, was a title of Roman emperors since 48 BC when a decree of the people of Ephesus declared Julius Caesar to be the 'universal savior of mankind'; thereafter it became a common title for the ruling Caesar" (Martin 1995, 164).

34. When Christ comes, what will happen to our earthly bodies (3:21)?

   • What amazing power will be used to change us (3:21b)? What confidence does that give you?

35. Mark the changes in our bodies/minds that will occur at our resurrection.

- Psalm 16:11 You make known to me the path of life; you will fill me with joy in your presence, with eternal pleasures at your right hand.

Digging Deeper
What does Revelation 21:4,5 add to these ideas? (What will happen to the harm caused by disease, genetic defects, injuries, age, etc.?)

- Job 19:26 "Even after my skin is destroyed, Yet from my flesh I will see God." NASB

- 1 Corinthians 13:12 Now we see but a poor reflection as in a mirror; then we shall see face to face. Now I know in part; then I shall know fully, even as I am fully known.

- 1 Corinthians 15:42–44 So will it be with the resurrection of the dead. The body that is sown is perishable, it is raised imperishable; it is sown in dishonor, it is raised in glory; it is sown in weakness, it is raised in power; it is sown a natural body, it is raised a spiritual body.

- 1 Corinthians 15:49 Just as we have borne the image of the earthy, we will also bear the image of the heavenly. NASB

- 1 Corinthians 15:52–53 ...the dead will be raised imperishable, and we will be changed. For the perishable must clothe itself with the imperishable, and the mortal with immortality.

- 1 John 3:2 Dear friends, now we are children of God, and what we will be has not yet been made known. But we know that when he appears, we shall be like him, for we shall see him as he is.

36. Underline how Christ's death on the cross for our salvation should affect our lives:

- 2 Corinthians 5:14–15 For Christ's love compels us, because we are convinced that one died for all, and therefore all died. [15] And he died for all, that those who live should no longer live for themselves but for him who died for them and was raised again.

- 2 Corinthians 3:18 And we all, who with unveiled faces contemplate the Lord's glory, are being transformed into his image with ever-increasing glory, which comes from the Lord, who is the Spirit.

- Romans 6:6 knowing this, that our old self was crucified with *Him*, in order that our body of sin might be done away with, so that we would no longer be slaves to sin. NAS

- 1 Peter 2:24 who Himself bore our sins in His own body on the tree, that we, having died to sins, might live for righteousness— NKJ

- 1 John 4:10–11 This is love: not that we loved God, but that he loved us and sent his Son as an atoning sacrifice for our sins. [11] Dear friends, since God so loved us, we also ought to love one another.

☙ **Applying the Word:** List some goals/priorities you have in life. How do they align with knowing Christ and the fact that you are a citizen of heaven?

Memory Verse:

"But one thing I do: Forgetting what is behind and straining toward what is ahead,
I press on toward the goal to win the prize
for which God has called me heavenward in Christ Jesus."
Philippians 3:13,14

☙

"Stand Firm in the Lord"

(4:1)

Philippians 4:1–9

Day 1
Relationships. Read Philippians 4:1–3

1. From 4:1, list the adjectives and titles Paul used of Philippian believers. See different translations. Compare 1:7–8.

   - What was his desire for them (4:1b)? See 2:2.

2. Why was Paul concerned for Euodia and Syntyche (4:2)? What needed to be the foundationally important for their relationship? Compare Romans 15:5–6.

   - How does his appeal for them relate to the command to "stand firm" in the Lord (4:1)? Compare 1:27.

   > **FYI: plead/beseech/entreat** "G3870 *parakaleo*; to call near, i.e. invite, invoke (by imploration, exhortation or consolation)" (Strong 2009, 1656).
   >
   > **live in harmony/agree/be of the same mind** "This is a far richer phrase in Greek than it is possible to translate into English. What he seeks is agreement in spirit and in attitude—a wholehearted, whole person sense of oneness" (Coleman and Peace 1988, 54).

3. What does the fact that Paul pleads with both women individually indicate about the problem and the responsibility each had? Notice that Paul did not take sides. If people in Philippi were taking sides, what was probably happening in this church? (See Galatians 5:15.)

4. To whom did Paul appeal in helping these women (4:3)?

   - What instructions from Philippians 2:1–5 would have guided them?

5. How had these women been involved in the ministry (4:3b)? What does that reveal about the difficulties and pressures they had been facing?

6. Read Romans 16:1–4,6,12–13,15. What would you say about the role of women in Paul's ministry?

7. Underline guidelines about resolving or avoiding conflicts:

   • Galatians 6:1–2 Brothers and sisters, if someone is caught in a sin, you who live by the Spirit should restore that person gently. But watch yourselves, or you also may be tempted. ² Carry each other's burdens, and in this way you will fulfill the law of Christ.

   • Colossians 3:13–14 Bear with each other and forgive one another if any of you has a grievance against someone. Forgive as the Lord forgave you. ¹⁴ And over all these virtues put on love, which binds them all together in perfect unity.

   • 1 Thessalonians 5:14–15 And we urge you, brothers and sisters, warn those who are idle and disruptive, encourage the disheartened, help the weak, be patient with everyone. ¹⁵ Make sure that nobody pays back wrong for wrong, but always strive to do what is good for each other and for everyone else.

   • 2 Timothy 2:23–25 Don't have anything to do with foolish and stupid arguments, because you know they produce quarrels. ²⁴ And the Lord's servant must not be quarrelsome but must be kind to everyone, able to teach, not resentful. ²⁵ Opponents must be gently instructed, in the hope that God will grant them repentance leading them to a knowledge of the truth.

8. Instead of finding fault, what did Paul remind everyone about? 4:3b Why would this be a powerful focus in the process of healing the conflict?

ෆ **Applying the Word:** What has this example said to you about any conflicts you have or see between other believers? What can you apply from Philippians 2:1–5 to help heal those relationships?

Do you know someone skilled at handling interpersonal conflicts? What helpful qualities do you see in them?

ෆ

9. What double command did Paul give next? 4:4 How does that relate to dealing with conflict? (Note: When are we to rejoice? In whom are we to rejoice?)

- What had the Philippians seen when Paul faced adversity? See Acts 16:22–25.

> **FYI:** "The Pauline appeals to joy are never simply encouragement; they throw back the distressed churches on their Lord; they are, above all, appeals to faith.' (Bonnard)" (Martin 1995, 170).

10. When Paul gave the command to "rejoice in the Lord always," what kinds of pressures/problems was Paul facing?

- 1:14

- 1:15–17

- 1:20

- 3:2

- 2:28; 4:2

> **Digging Deeper**
> Review the issues Paul connected with rejoicing:
>
> 1:4 *prayers for others*
>
> 1:18
>
> 1:25
>
> 2:2
>
> 2:17
>
> 3:1
>
> 4:1
>
> 4:10

11. What can trials produce?

- 1 Peter 1:6–9

- James 1:2–4

- Romans 5:2–5

12. Do you see a difference between "rejoicing in the Lord" versus being happy? Compare 2 Corinthians 6:10.

13. What other attitude did Paul encourage believers to have (4:5)?

- What does the word "all" say about this responsibility? (See Titus 3:2.)

> **FYI: gentle spirit/gentleness** "L. H. Marshall gives a full description of its meaning as 'fairmindedness, the attitude of a man who is charitable towards men's faults and merciful in his judgment of their failings because he takes their whole situation into his reckoning.'" (Martin 1995, 170).
>
> "This is the attitude of 'graciousness' or 'magnanimity' which is shown in situations when one could legitimately stand on one's 'rights' and yet, for the sake of the other, does not insist on these rights" (Coleman and Peace 1988, 55).

14. How do you think gentleness (also translated as reasonableness, graciousness, considerate, and patient) affects anger or conflict? See Proverbs 15:1,18.

15. In the following verses, underline the things connected with gentleness.

- James 3:17 But the wisdom from above is first pure, then peaceable, gentle, reasonable, full of mercy and good fruits, unwavering, without hypocrisy. NASB

- 2 Timothy 2:24–25 And the Lord's servant must not be quarrelsome but must be kind to everyone, able to teach, not resentful. 25 Opponents must be gently instructed, in the hope that God will grant them repentance leading them to a knowledge of the truth.

- 1 Peter 3:15–16 But in your hearts revere Christ as Lord. Always be prepared to give an answer to everyone who asks you to give the reason for the hope that you have. But do this with gentleness and respect, 16 keeping a clear conscience, so that those who speak maliciously against your good behavior in Christ may be ashamed of their slander.

16. When and why should we exercise gentleness?

- Romans 12:17–21

- Ephesians 4:32

> **FYI:** "When we let our 'gentle spirit' shine through in our words, attitudes, and actions, it will have a transformative effect on our hearts and minds" (Swindoll 2017, 136).

17. How did the Lord describe Himself (Matthew 11:29–30)?

- How has He treated us? See Psalm 103:8–14.

18. How would the reminder that "the Lord is near" (4:5b)—which could mean His presence or His coming—encourage gentleness? (Compare 2 Thessalonians 1:7ff)

℘ **Applying the Word:** Can you think of a time when someone treated you with gentleness even though you didn't deserve it? How did that impact you? Have you passed it on?

℘

Day 3
Prayer. Read Philippians 4:6–7

19. What two contrasting behaviors are given in 4:6? Why are they opposed to each other?

> **FYI:** "Every time we begin to **worry**, we should see that as a call from God telling us that it's time to pray...The sobering truth is that the more you worry, the less you pray. But the more you pray, the less you worry" (Evans 2019, 1411).
>
> "We are to worry about nothing, because we can pray about everything!" (Morris 1995, 1319).

20. How comprehensive should our prayers be? (Note the words "always, all, anything, every" in 4:4–7.) What does this say about God's interest in our concerns?

21. Why should "thanksgiving" be an integral part of prayer and supplication? How do you think gratitude affects our prayer life?

    • What thought does 1 Thessalonians 5:18 add to this? See David's attitude in Psalm 145:1–2.

> **FYI:** "Pagan prayers are destitute of thanksgiving (cf. Romans 1:21; 2 Timothy 3:2), whereas truly Christian prayer breathes thanksgiving because thankfulness is the posture of grace... thanksgiving for what God has done for us in Christ through the gospel" (Hughes 2007, 169).
>
> "The recalling of God's goodness and mercy will save us from the many pitfalls which await the ungrateful soul, e.g. over-concern with or immediate problems, forgetfulness of God's gracious dealings with us in the past, disregard of the needs of others who are less fortunate than we are" (Martin 1995, 172).

22. Since God already knows our requests (Psalm 139:4) before we pray them, what reason do you see in making them "known to God" (4:6)? What does that do to our hearts, our minds, and any anxiety we have? What does it do for our relationship with Him?

23. In Matthew 6:25–34, what reasons did Jesus give for why we shouldn't worry?

24. What did Jesus say about how our anxiety affects our productivity (Matthew 13:22)?

> **FYI:** "Worry involves imagining the future in a worst-case scenario and then freaking out about it...Do you live with self-defeating, persistent thoughts filled with worry? This type of anxiety, which Jesus and Paul talk about, is sin. This form of worry is pagan; it could be called 'functional atheism' because you're living as though God doesn't exist, as if He's not the all-sovereign ruler over all...Crushing anxiety happens when I believe lies. You might think of your worries as false prophets. They're telling you that God isn't good, sovereign, and wise" (Merida and Chan 2016, 175).

25. If we cast our cares on the Lord, what promise are we given (4:7)?

- What does "surpasses all understanding/comprehension" say about the dimensions of this peace? Compare 2 Thessalonians 3:16.

26. What picture does the idea of a garrison or guard (a military term) give you? See Psalm 32:6,7 and 139:5.

> **Digging Deeper**
> From Romans 5:1, how do we have "peace **with** God"?
>
> How was this peace obtained? See Colossians 1:19–20.
>
> What kind of peace did Jesus say He offers in John 14:27?

> **FYI: guard** "G5432 *phroureo*; to be a watcher in advance, i.e. to mount guard as a sentinel (post spies at gates); figuratively, to hem in, protect:— keep (with a garrison)" (Strong 2009, 1682).

27. Underline other ways describing how peace is found.

- Isaiah 26:3 You will keep him in perfect peace, Whose mind is stayed on You, Because he trusts in You. NKJV

- Romans 8:6 The mind of sinful man is death, but the mind controlled by the Spirit is life and peace.

- Romans 15:13 May the God of hope fill you with all joy and peace as you trust in him, so that you may overflow with hope by the power of the Holy Spirit.

- 2 Peter 1:2 Grace and peace be yours in abundance through the knowledge of God and of Jesus our Lord.

28. Read "Cast All Your Cares on Him" at the end of this lesson. Mark anything that is meaningful or helpful. Which verse do you need to claim or think about today?

ଓ **Applying the Word:** "Fight all your battles on your knees, and you win every time." (Charles Stanley) Are you feeling anxious, sad, tired, frustrated, or angry about anything? Say or write out a prayer to the Lord about it using Philippians 4:6–8 as a guide.

ଓ

Day 4
Thought Life. Read Philippians 4:8–9

29. From the list in 4:8, how would you summarize the mindset and attitudes that Paul instructed believers to have?

- Why is this more than positive thinking?

- What mindset will help us do that (Colossians 3:1–3)?

> **FYI: think about/dwell on** "*logizomai* (3049),...it signifies 'make those things the subjects of your thoughtful consideration,' or 'carefully reflect on them' (RV marg., 'take account of')" (Vine 1985, 628).

30. Mark other instructions that are given about our mindset in the following verses.

- Romans 12 2 Do not conform to the pattern of this world, but be transformed by the renewing of your mind. Then you will be able to test and approve what God's will is—his good, pleasing and perfect will.

- Ephesians 4:23–24 Be made new in the attitude of your minds; 24 and to put on the new self, created to be like God in true righteousness and holiness.

- 1 Peter 1:13 So prepare your minds for action and exercise self-control. Put all your hope in the gracious salvation that will come to you when Jesus Christ is revealed to the world. NLT

- Mark 12:29–30 "The most important one," answered Jesus, "is this: 'Hear, O Israel: The Lord our God, the Lord is one. 30 Love the Lord your God with all your heart and with all your soul and with all your mind and with all your strength.' 31 The second is this: 'Love your neighbor as yourself.' There is no commandment greater than these."

31. Why do you think the list starts with whatever is "true"?

- Who/what is described as truth in John 3:33; 14:16, 17 and 17:17?

32. In what ways do you think our culture would change if we valued these characteristics?

> **FYI:** "Everything that is true is from God because all truth is God's truth. A mind that contemplates what is true not only sees Christ, the Word, and the gospel but also ... seeks 'whatever is true' in every avenue of life, from faith to science to relationships to public life to business" (Hughes 2007, 175).

33. Read 4:8 substituting opposite words in the list: "Whatever is false, whatever is dishonorable..."). What keeps you in these negative thoughts rather than the ones listed in 4:8?

Digging Deeper
What kind of thoughts will characterize people in the "last days" according to 2 Timothy 3:1–5?

What happened in the days of Noah? See Genesis 6:5.

- How is replacing negative thoughts with the positive thoughts given in 4:8 more powerful than ignoring or fighting them?

> **FYI:** "One of the reasons we don't keep our peace is that we tend to dwell on the things that are set in opposition to the peace we're asking for. If we continue to entertain messages that work against our peace, anxiety will soon return. We must, therefore, ask ourselves if we are able to praise God for the things that we are dwelling on. If we can't, then we'll soon lose the peace God has given us" (Evans 2019, 1411).

34. How powerful is the warfare that we wage with our thoughts? See Proverbs 23:7a (KJV or NAS) and Luke 6:45.

- From 2 Corinthians 10:3–5, what kind of strength does it take to set our minds on the right thoughts?

35. How does walking with the Lord need to go beyond thoughts and prayers (4:9)? What promise accompanies this?

FYI: practice/do "G4238 *prasso*; to 'practice', i.e. perform repeatedly or habitually" (Strong 2009, 1662).

Whatever things..."learned from the teachings of Paul (and others in the church); from the revelation of God (in the Old Testament and in the teachings of Jesus); and by what they hear and see in Paul's life" (Coleman and Peace 1988, 55).

"Before they were committed to writing and later formed the corpus of New Testament scripture they were learned, received, heard, seen in the person of the apostles" (Martin 1995, 175).

[For what had been learned and seen, see 1 Cor. 15:1–2ff; Colossians 2:6; 1 Thess. 4:1–2ff; 2 Thess. 2:15.]

36. How do the promises about peace in 4:7 and 4:9b compare? What combined assurance do they give?

FYI: "We have 'peace with God' (Romans 5:1) and the 'peace of God,' when we know 'the God of peace' (Philippians 4:9)" (Morris 1995, 1319).

"We can have a contagious, deep-seated joy when we have confidence that Christ is in full control —not just of the big things, but of the little things as well" (Swindoll 2017, 143).

37. Which of the commands in 4:4–9 do you think you need to focus on to find peace?

☙ **Applying the Word:** Think of a circumstance or person with whom you are struggling. List some things that are true, honorable, right, pure, virtuous, etc. about that person or situation. How does that change your perspective?

What makes it hard for you to keep your thought life on the things Paul lists in 4:8? Using this list, how would you rate the things you watch in the media, things you read, and conversations you have? How should purity affect all areas of our lives (words, actions, thoughts, motives)?

Keywords in Chapter 4
joy (rejoice)
in the Lord (in Christ Jesus
peace
things

CB

"Cast All Your Cares On Him"

- Deuteronomy 33:27 The eternal God is your refuge, and his everlasting arms are under you. NLT

- Psalm 18:1–2 I love you, O LORD, my strength. ² The LORD is my rock, my fortress and my deliverer; my God is my rock, in whom I take refuge. He is my shield and the horn of my salvation, my stronghold.

- Psalm 55:22 Cast your cares on the LORD and he will sustain you; he will never let the righteous fall.

- Psalm 103:11 For as high as the heavens are above the earth, so great is his love for those who fear him.

- Isaiah 26:3–4 You will keep in perfect peace him whose mind is steadfast, because he trusts in you. ⁴ Trust in the LORD forever, for the LORD, the LORD, is the Rock eternal.

- Isaiah 40:28–31 Do you not know? Have you not heard? The LORD is the everlasting God, the Creator of the ends of the earth. He will not grow tired or weary, and his understanding no one can fathom. ²⁹ He gives strength to the weary and increases the power of the weak. ³⁰ Even youths grow tired and weary, and young men stumble and fall; ³¹ but those who hope in the LORD will renew their strength. They will soar on wings like eagles; they will run and not grow weary, they will walk and not be faint.

- Isaiah 41:10 "So do not fear, for I am with you; do not be dismayed, for I am your God. I will strengthen you and help you; I will uphold you with my righteous right hand."

- Jeremiah 32:27 "I am the LORD, the God of all mankind. Is anything too hard for me?

- Luke 12:6–7 Are not five sparrows sold for two pennies? Yet not one of them is forgotten by God. ⁷ Indeed, the very hairs of your head are all numbered. Don't be afraid; you are worth more than many sparrows.

- Romans 8:15 For you did not receive a spirit that makes you a slave again to fear, but you received the Spirit of sonship. And by him we cry, "Abba, Father."

- Romans 8:26–27 In the same way, the Spirit helps us in our weakness. We do not know what we ought to pray for, but the Spirit himself intercedes for us with groans that words cannot express. ²⁷ And he who searches our hearts knows the mind of the Spirit, because the Spirit intercedes for the saints in accordance with God's will.

- Romans 8:28 And we know that in all things God works for the good of those who love him, who have been called according to his purpose.

- Romans 8:37–39 No, in all these things we are more than conquerors through him who loved us. [38] For I am convinced that neither death nor life, neither angels nor demons, neither the present nor the future, nor any powers, [39] neither height nor depth, nor anything else in all creation, will be able to separate us from the love of God that is in Christ Jesus our Lord.

- 1 Corinthians 10:13 No temptation has seized you except what is common to man. And God is faithful; he will not let you be tempted beyond what you can bear. But when you are tempted, he will also provide a way out so that you can stand up under it.

- Ephesians 3:16 I pray that out of his glorious riches he may strengthen you with power through his Spirit in your inner being.

- Ephesians 3:20 Now to him who is able to do immeasurably more than all we ask or imagine, according to his power that is at work within us.

- 1 Thessalonians 5:24 The one who calls you is faithful and he will do it.

- 2 Thessalonians 3:3 But the Lord is faithful, and he will strengthen and protect you from the evil one.

- 2 Timothy 1:7 For God hath not given us the spirit of fear; but of power, and of love, and of a sound mind. KJV

- Hebrews 4:15–16 For we do not have a high priest who is unable to sympathize with our weaknesses, but we have one who has been tempted in every way, just as we are—yet was without sin. [16] Let us then approach the throne of grace with confidence, so that we may receive mercy and find grace to help us in our time of need.

- Hebrews 13:5–6 Keep your lives free from the love of money and be content with what you have, because God has said, "Never will I leave you; never will I forsake you." [6] So we say with confidence, "The Lord is my helper; I will not be afraid. What can man do to me?"

- 1 Peter 5:6–7 Humble yourselves, therefore, under God's mighty hand, that he may lift you up in due time. [7] Cast all your anxiety on him because he cares for you.

- 2 Peter 1:3 His divine power has given us everything we need for life and godliness through our knowledge of him who called us by his own glory and goodness.

"Through Christ Who Strengthens Me"

(4:13)

Philippians 4:10–23

Day 1
Contentment. Read Philippians 4:10–14

1. What had been "revived/renewed" by the Philippians (4:10)? What do you think may have prevented or delayed their opportunity to give again?

2. What did Paul say about his circumstances (4:11)? What comfort would this have given them?

3. List the contrasts Paul gave in 4:12.

   • By saying he had "learned," what would you say about contentment?

   • How can either of these extremes threaten a person's ministry?

4. How does 2 Corinthians 12:7–10 describe a process Paul went through in learning contentment?

5. What was Paul's "secret" for confidence and contentment (4:13)?

> **FYI:** "The 'all things' refers to surviving the extremes of life. To paraphrase: 'Whatever ups and downs life sends my way, I can handle whatever comes, not through my own strength, but by the power of Christ'" (Swindoll 2017, 146).
>
> "This is the secret: Christ is enough. Christ empowers us to be content...Paul isn't preoccupied with his situation; he's preoccupied with Jesus. This is the secret" (Merida and Chan 2016, 191–192).
>
> "The beginning of contentment in all circumstances of life, I believe, is the realization of two facts. First, God controls all the circumstances of life. Secondly, this God, Who controls or rules as Sovereign Ruler over the whole universe, loves us and promises us that everything will result in good to conform us to the image of His Son (Romans 8:28–29)" (Arthur 1976, 94).

6. From 1 Corinthians 4:11–13, list some hardships Paul endured and how he responded.

7. How did Paul compliment the Philippians for their gift (4:14)? Compare 1:4–5.

8. Mark what is said in the following about contentment and generosity.

   • 1 Timothy 6:6–8 But godliness with contentment is great gain. ⁷ For we brought nothing into the world, and we can take nothing out of it. ⁸ But if we have food and clothing, we will be content with that.

   • 1 Timothy 6:17–18 Command those who are rich in this present world not to be arrogant nor to put their hope in wealth, which is so uncertain, but to put their hope in God, who richly provides us with everything for our enjoyment. ¹⁸ Command them to do good, to be rich in good deeds, and to be generous and willing to share.

> **Digging Deeper**
> What is the point of the parable that Jesus told about riches (Luke 12:16–21)?

   • Hebrews 13:5 Keep your lives free from the love of money and be content with what you have, because God has said, "Never will I leave you; never will I forsake you."

   • Ephesians 4:28 Anyone who has been stealing must steal no longer, but must work, doing something useful with their own hands, that they may have something to share with those in need.

9. How had Paul often paid for his ministry? See Acts 18:2–3.

10. In the following verse, record the reasons Paul gave for not asking for financial support from the churches he ministered to.

   • Acts 20:33–35

   • 1 Thessalonians 2:9

   • 2 Thessalonians 3:7–10

11. From 1 Corinthians 9:9–18, how did Paul feel about a missionary/minister's financial support? Why did he refuse their support (9:12)?

ɔ🙰 **Applying the Word:** What are some of the best lessons in life that have taught you to depend on the Lord and be content with what you have or where you are?

ɔ🙰

12. In what were the Philippians "sharing" (4:14)?

- How faithful had the Philippians been in supporting Paul in his travels (4:15,16)? Since Paul was in jail, and possibly in Rome when he received their gift, what does that say about their determination to support him?

- What excuses could the Philippians have given for not supporting him after he left their city and ministered in another?

> FYI: **more than once** "The Philippians had begun donating to the cause immediately...and continued to donate repeatedly. Their partnership with Paul was both early and enduring. Their generosity overflowed" (Swindoll 2017, 146).

13. When writing to the church in Corinth (a very wealthy city), how did Paul describe the Philippians and their giving (2 Corinthians 8:1–5; 11:9)?

- What did he call the work of giving (2 Corinthians 8:7)?

- What example have we been given (2 Corinthians 8:9)?

- How did Paul describe God's gift to us (2 Corinthians 9:15)?

> FYI: "We give because we are saved, not in order to be saved. We give as a response to the marvelous grace that God has shown us. We give because Jesus is a giver!" (Merida and Chan 2016, 196).

14. What pleased Paul the most about their gift (4:17)?

- What kind of "profit/fruit/credit" do you think Paul was referring to? Compare 2 Corinthians 9:12 and Ephesians 6:8.

15. From 4:18a, list the terms Paul used to describe how he had been supplied.

- List the terms that describe what these gifts were to God (4:18b). (See Numbers 15:3.) What value and motivation does this impart to giving?

16. In the following verses, mark principles about giving.

- Proverbs 11:25 A generous person will prosper; whoever refreshes others will be refreshed.

- Acts 20:35 "In everything I did, I showed you that by this kind of hard work we must help the weak, remembering the words the Lord Jesus himself said: 'It is more blessed to give than to receive.'"

- 2 Corinthians 8:12 For if the willingness is there, the gift is acceptable according to what one has, not according to what one does not have.

- 2 Corinthians 9:6–7 Remember this: Whoever sows sparingly will also reap sparingly, and whoever sows generously will also reap generously. ^{7} Each of you should give what you have decided in your heart to give, not reluctantly or under compulsion, for God loves a cheerful giver.

- 1 John 3:17–18 If anyone has material possessions and sees a brother or sister in need but has no pity on them, how can the love of God be in that person? ^{18} Dear children, let us not love with words or speech but with actions and in truth.

17. In the following verses, underline the effects of greed.

- Proverbs 11:28 Whoever trusts in his riches will fall, but the righteous will thrive like a green leaf.

- Prov. 15:27 A greedy man brings trouble to his family, but he who hates bribes will live.

- Ecclesiastes 5:10–11 Whoever loves money never has money enough; whoever loves wealth is never satisfied with his income. This too is meaningless. ^{11} As goods increase, so do those who consume them. And what benefit are they to the owners except to feast their eyes on them?

- Ecclesiastes 5:13 I have seen a grievous evil under the sun: wealth hoarded to the harm of its owner

- Matthew 13:22 "The one who received the seed that fell among the thorns is the man who hears the word, but the worries of this life and the deceitfulness of wealth choke it, making it unfruitful."

- Matthew 6:19–24 "Do not store up for yourselves treasures on earth...²⁰ But store up for yourselves treasures in heaven, where moths and vermin do not destroy, and where thieves do not break in and steal. ²¹ For where your treasure is, there your heart will be also...²⁴ No one can serve two masters. Either you will hate the one and love the other, or you will be devoted to the one and despise the other. You cannot serve both God and money."

> **Digging Deeper**
> How did Zacchaeus's life change when he met Jesus? See Luke 19:5–10.

- 1 Timothy 6:9–10 People who want to get rich fall into temptation and a trap and into many foolish and harmful desires that plunge men into ruin and destruction. ¹⁰ For the love of money is a root of all kinds of evil. Some people, eager for money, have wandered from the faith and pierced themselves with many griefs.

ය **Applying the Word:** What are some loving and creative ways that you have seen people be generous in giving (financially or through other means)?

ය

18. On what promise can we rely (4:19)? What kinds of "needs" besides financial would this include?

    • From 4:19b, write out the phrase describing what God's supply is "according to." How vast is this?

19. What do the words "all" and "needs" indicate about God's care and faithfulness?

    • What is said in 2 Corinthians 9:8?

    > **FYI: your needs** "That is, 'your business,' or necessities for the business of the kingdom. Those who freely give will also receive (like the Philippians)—not their wants, but all they need for their service for Christ" (Morris 1995, 1320).
    >
    > "'In Christ' is the most used description of the believer in Paul's letters...Paul began this letter...'To the saints in Christ Jesus (1:1) and concluded 'in Christ Jesus.' For Christians, every need is met in Christ. He is our beginning and our end. All things come to us in Him and through Him" (Hughes 2007, 186,194).

20. Read through Philippians 4:19 out loud several times. The first time, emphasize the first word or phrase: "**And my God** will meet all your needs according to the riches of His glory in Christ Jesus." The second time, emphasize the second word or phrase. The third time, the third word or phrase—and so on throughout the verse." How did that impact you?

21. How would you explain God's ability to meet all our needs but His desire for believers to help meet each other's needs? See Galatians 6:2.

22. Underline the "riches" of God named in the following verses.

    • Romans 2:4 Or do you show contempt for the <u>riches of his kindness, tolerance, and patience</u>, not realizing that God's kindness leads you toward repentance?

- Romans 11:33–36 Oh, the depth of the riches of the wisdom and knowledge of God! How unsearchable his judgments, and his paths beyond tracing out! [34] "Who has known the mind of the Lord? Or who has been his counselor? [35] Who has ever given to God, that God should repay them?" [36] For from him and through him and for him are all things. To him be the glory forever! Amen.

- Ephesians 1:7–8 In him we have redemption through his blood, the forgiveness of sins, in accordance with the riches of God's grace [8] that he lavished on us with all wisdom and understanding.

- Ephesians 1:18 I pray also that the eyes of your heart may be enlightened in order that you may know the hope to which he has called you, the riches of his glorious inheritance in the saints

- Ephesians 2:6–7 And God raised us up with Christ and seated us with him in the heavenly realms in Christ Jesus, [7] in order that in the coming ages he might show the incomparable riches of his grace, expressed in his kindness to us in Christ Jesus.

- Ephesians 3:8 Although I am less than the least of all God's people, this grace was given me: to preach to the Gentiles the unsearchable riches of Christ,

- Ephesians 3:16–17 I pray that out of his glorious riches he may strengthen you with power through his Spirit in your inner being, [17] so that Christ may dwell in your hearts through faith.

- Colossians 1:27 To them God has chosen to make known among the Gentiles the glorious riches of this mystery, which is Christ in you, the hope of glory.

- Colossians 2:2–3 My goal is that they may be encouraged in heart and united in love, so that they may have the full riches of complete understanding, in order that they may know the mystery of God, namely, Christ, [3] in whom are hidden all the treasures of wisdom and knowledge.

23. Read through the **"In Christ"** verses at the end of the lesson. Mark things that are meaningful to you. Are there any blessings that you have never claimed?

24. What did thoughts of God's loving care cause Paul to do (4:20)? Compare Jude 1:24–25.

C3 **Applying the Word:** What are some daily practices/habits that help you to be mindful of Christ's presence? What is something you are struggling with today? What is one step (one thought or action) you could take to seek His presence, power, and peace?

C3

Day 4
Farewells. Read Philippians 4:21–23

25. What do Paul's closing remarks indicate about the community of believers and the nature of Paul's ministry (4:21,22)?

> **FYI: Caesar's household** "Not blood relatives of the emperor, but those employed (slaves or freedmen) in or around the palace area (cf. 'palace guard,' 1:13)" (Barker 1985, 1810).
>
> **greet** (4:21) "G782 *aspazomai;* to enfold in the arms, i.e. (by implication) to salute, (figuratively) to welcome:— embrace, greet, salute, take leave" (Strong 2009, 1610).

26. Review the ways Paul and the Philippians had fellowshipped/shared/partnered together.

    • 1:5

    • 1:7

    • 2:1,4

    • 4:14

    • 4:15

27. What do you think Paul's blessing at the end means (4:23)? (Compare other endings to Paul's letters such as 2 Timothy 4:22 and 2 Corinthians 13:14.)

28. List the things Paul associates with being "in Christ, in the Lord" or "through Him" in Philippians 4.

    • 4:1

    • 4:2

    • 4:4,10

    • 4:7

    • 4:13

    • 4:19

    • 4:21

29. Paul's letter begins (1:2) and ends (4:23) with a focus on God's grace. How is that a picture of the Christian life?

> **FYI: grace** (4:23) "5485. *charis;...*to rejoice. Grace, particularly that which causes joy, pleasure, gratification, favor acceptance, for a kindness granted or desired, a benefit, thanks, gratitude. A favor done without expectation of return' the absolutely free expression of the loving kindness of God to men finding its only motive in the bounty and benevolence of the Giver; unearned and unmerited favor" (Zodhiates 1992, 1469).

30. Look through the letter to the Philippians, and list some of the ways that God has "graced" us. (For example see: 1:6,11; 2:1,13; 3:9; 4:7,13,19.)

31. Read Romans 8:31–39. How gracious is the Lord with us?

32. In the following, underline things associated with grace.

- Hebrews 4:16 Let us then approach God's throne of grace with confidence, so that we may receive mercy and find grace to help us in our time of need.

- 1 Corinthians 1:4–5 I always thank my God for you because of his grace given you in Christ Jesus. [5] For in him you have been enriched in every way—with all kinds of speech and with all knowledge—

- 1 Corinthians 15:10 But by the grace of God I am what I am, and his grace to me was not without effect. No, I worked harder than all of them—yet not I, but the grace of God that was with me.

- Ephesians 1:7–8 In him we have redemption through his blood, the forgiveness of sins, in accordance with the riches of God's grace [8] that he lavished on us. With all wisdom and understanding,

- Ephesians 2:4–9 But because of his great love for us, God, who is rich in mercy, [5] made us alive with Christ even when we were dead in transgressions—it is by grace you have been saved [6] And God raised us up with Christ and seated us with him in the heavenly realms in Christ Jesus, [7] in order that in the coming ages he might show the incomparable riches of his grace, expressed in his kindness to us in Christ Jesus. [8] For it is by grace you have been saved, through faith—and this is not from yourselves, it is the gift of God— [9] not by works, so that no one can boast.

- Titus 2:11–12 For the grace of God has appeared that offers salvation to all people. [12] It teaches us to say "No" to ungodliness and worldly passions, and to live self-controlled, upright and godly lives in this present age,

 C෪ **Applying the Word:** What is one of the most meaningful truths/assurances/promises you will take away from studying Philippians?

Memory Verses:
"I can do all things through Christ who strengthens me."
Philippians 4:13 NKJ

"And my God will supply all your needs
according to His riches in glory in Christ Jesus. ."
Philippians 4:19 NASB

C෪

IN CHRIST:

You are forgiven:
Ephesians 1:7 In him we have redemption through his blood, the forgiveness of sins, in accordance with the riches of God's grace.

You are justified:
Romans 4:25 He was delivered over to death for our sins and was raised to life for our justification.

You are at peace with God:
Romans 5:1 Therefore, since we have been justified through faith, we have peace with God through our Lord Jesus Christ.

You are saved from wrath:
Romans 5:9–10 Since we have now been justified by his blood, how much more shall we be saved from God's wrath through him! [10] For if, when we were God's enemies, we were reconciled to him through the death of his Son, how much more, having been reconciled, shall we be saved through his life!

You are not condemned:
Rom 8:1 Therefore, there is now no condemnation for those who are in Christ Jesus,

Ephesians 1:4 He chose us in Him before the foundation of the world that we should be holy and blameless before Him. NAS

You have free access to God:
Ephesians 2:18 For through him we both have access to the Father by one Spirit.

Ephesians 3:12 In him and through faith in him we may approach God with freedom and confidence.

Hebrews 4:16 Let us then approach the throne of grace with confidence, so that we may receive mercy and find grace to help us in our time of need.

Hebrews 10:19–20 Therefore, brothers, since we have confidence to enter the Most Holy Place by the blood of Jesus, [20] by a new and living way opened for us through the curtain, that is, his body.

You are loved and cared for:
Colossians 3:12 Therefore, as God's chosen people, holy and dearly loved, clothe yourselves with compassion, kindness, humility, gentleness and patience.

1 Pet 5:7 Cast all your anxiety on him because he cares for you.

Hebrews 13:5–6 …God has said, "Never will I leave you; never will I forsake you." [6] So we say with confidence, "The Lord is my helper; I will not be afraid. What can man do to me?"

You are complete in Him:
Colossians 2:9–10 For in Him all the fulness of Deity dwells in bodily form, [10] and in Him you have been made complete, and He is the head over all rule and authority. NAS

You have His life in you:
Galatians 2:20 I have been crucified with Christ; and it is no longer I who live, but Christ lives in me; and the life which I now live in the flesh I live by faith in the Son of God, who loved me, and delivered Himself up for me. NAS

Colossians 1:27 To them God has chosen to make known among the Gentiles the glorious riches of this mystery, which is Christ in you, the hope of glory.

You have His righteousness:
1 Corinthians 1:30 It is because of him that you are in Christ Jesus, who has become for us wisdom from God— that is, our righteousness, holiness and redemption.

2 Corinthians 5:21 God made him who had no sin to be sin for us, so that in him we might become the righteousness of God.

Philippians 3:9 And may be found in him, not having a righteousness of my own derived from the law, but that which is through faith in Christ, the righteousness which comes from God on the basis of faith. NAS

You are a new creation:
2 Corinthians 5:17 Therefore, if anyone is in Christ, he is a new creation; the old has gone, the new has come!

1 Corinthians 6:11 And that is what some of you were. But you were washed, you were sanctified, you were justified in the name of the Lord Jesus Christ and by the Spirit of our God.

Titus 3:4–6 But when the kindness and love of God our Savior appeared, [5] he saved us, not because of righteous things we had done, but because of his mercy. He saved us through the washing of rebirth and renewal by the Holy Spirit, [6] whom he poured out on us generously through Jesus Christ our Savior.

Your inheritance is guaranteed:
2 Corinthians 1:21–22 Now it is God who makes both us and you stand firm in Christ. He anointed us, [2] set his seal of ownership on us, and put his Spirit in our hearts as a deposit, guaranteeing what is to come.

Ephesians 1:13–14 In Him you also trusted, after you heard the word of truth, the gospel of your salvation; in whom also, having believed, you were sealed with the Holy Spirit of promise, [14] who is the guarantee of our inheritance until the redemption of the purchased possession, to the praise of His glory. NKJ

You are blessed with heavenly blessings:
Ephesians 1:3 Praise be to the God and Father of our Lord Jesus Christ, who has blessed us in the heavenly realms with every spiritual blessing in Christ.

You have been raised and seated in the heavenly realms:
Colossians 3:1–4 Since, then, you have been raised with Christ, set your hearts on things above, where Christ is seated at the right hand of God. [2] Set your minds on things above, not on earthly things. [3] For you died, and your life is now hidden with Christ in God. [4] When Christ, who is your life, appears, then you also will appear with him in glory.

Ephesians 2:6–7 And God raised us up with Christ and seated us with him in the heavenly realms in Christ Jesus, [7] in order that in the coming ages he might show the incomparable riches of his grace, expressed in his kindness to us in Christ Jesus.

References

Arthur, Kay. *Philippians: How to Have Joy No Matter What, Precept Upon Precept*. Reach Out, Inc. 1976.

Barry, John D., ed. *NIV Faithlife Study Bible: Intriguing insights to inform your faith*. Grand Rapids, MI: Zondervan, 2017.

Barton, Bruce B., Dave Veerman, Linda K. Taylor, and Mark Fackler. *Life Application Bible Commentary: Philippians, Colossians, Philemon*. Edited by Philip Wesley Comfort. Wheaton, IL: Tyndale House Publishers, 1995.

Barker, Kenneth L., ed. *The NIV Study Bible: New International Version*. Grand Rapids, MI: Zondervan Pub. House, 1985.

Biblesoft's New Exhaustive Strong's Numbers and Concordance with Expanded Greek and Hebrew Dictionary. Seattle: Biblesoft and International Bible Translators, Inc. 1994. Software.

Ray Burns. "3 Reasons Legalism is so Appealing." Onward in the Faith. July 16, 2019. https://onwardinthefaith.com/3-reasons-legalism-is-so-appealing/.

Coleman, Lyman, and Richard Peace. *Study Guide for the Book of Philippians, Mastering the Basics*. Serendipity House, 1988.

Easton, Matthew George. "Timothy - Easton's Bible Dictionary Online." Bible Study Tools. Accessed January 30, 2024. https://www.biblestudytools.com/dictionaries/eastons-bible-dictionary/timothy.html.

Evans, Tony. *Holy Bible: CSB Tony Evans Study Bible*. Holman Bible Pub, 2019.

Guzik, David. "Enduring Word Bible Commentary: Philippians." Enduring Word. Accessed 2023. https://enduringword.com/bible-commentary/philippians-1/

Gaebelein, Frank E. and J.D. Douglas, eds. *The Expositor's Bible Commentary with the New International Version: Volume 11 Ephesians - Philemon*. Grand Rapids, MI: Zondervan Pub. House, 1978.

——— *The Expositor's Bible Commentary with the New International Version: Volume 9 John - Acts*. Grand Rapids, MI: Zondervan Pub. House, 1981.

Garland, Tony. "Commentaries on Philippians." Precept Austin. Accessed January 25, 2024. https://www.preceptaustin.org/bybook/50

GotQuestions. "What is Antinomianism?" GotQuestions.org. August 14, 2007. https://www. gotquestions.org/antinomianism.html.

Hughes, R. Kent. *Philippians: The Fellowship of the Gospel.* Wheaton, IL: Crossway, 2009.

Johnson, Phil. "Truth & Love: Inseparable Virtues." Answers in Genesis. March 30, 2022. https://answersingenesis.org/the-word-of-god/truth-love-insepa rable-virtues/.

Lee-Thorp, Karen, ed. *A life-changing encounter with god's word from the book of Philippians. Life Change Series.* Colorado Springs, CO: NavPress, 1987.

Ligonier Ministries, 2023 "Ligonier Editorial What Are Legalism and Antinomianism?"

Ligonier.org. April 5, 2023. https://www.ligonier.org/learn/articles/field-guide-on-false-teaching-legalism-antinomianism.

Martin, Ralph P. *Tydale New Testament Commentaries: Philippians.* Grand Rapids, MI: Inter-Varsity Press, 1994.

Merida, Tony, Francis Chan, David Platt, and Daniel L. Akin. *Exalting Jesus in Philippians.* Holman Reference, 2016.

Miller, Chris. "Old Testament Literature." Cedarville University. Accessed 2023. https://www.cedarville.edu/academic-schools-and-departments/biblical-and-theological-studies/bible-minor-project/old-testament-literature.

Morris, Henry M. *The Defender's Study Bible: King James Version.* Grand Rapids, MI: World Pub., 1995.

——— "He Became Poor." The Institute for Creation Research. July 13, 2023. https://www. icr.org/article/1411.

——— "The Name above Every Name." The Institute for Creation Research. September 17, 2023. https://www.icr.org/article/above-every-name/.

——— "The Whole Law." The Institute for Creation Research, January 3, 1996. https://www. icr.org/article/1992).

NIV Archaeological Study Bible: An illustrated walk through biblical history and culture: New international version. Grand Rapids, MI: Zondervan, 2005.

Stedman, Ray. 2024. "Riches in Christ: God at Work." Ray Stedman.org. Accessed January 19, 2024 https://www.raystedman.org/new-testament/ephesians/god-at-work

Strong, James. *Strong's exhaustive concordance of the Bible.* Peabody, MA: Hendrickson Pub., 2009.

Storms, Sam. "What Does It Mean to Worship God in Spirit and Truth?" The Gospel Coalition, March 14, 2020. Accessed January, 2024 https://www.thegospel coalition.org/article/what-does-it-mean-to-worship-god-in-spirit-and-truth/.

Swindoll, Charles R. *Swindoll's Living Insights on Philippians, Colossians, Philemon.* Carol Stream, IL: Tyndale House Publishers, Inc., 2017.

Vine, W. E., Merrill F. Unger, and William White. *Vine's Complete Expository Dictionary of Old and New Testament Words.* Nashville, TN: T. Nelson, 1985.

Zodhiates, Spiros. *The Complete Word Study Dictionary: New Testament.* Chattanooga, TN: Publishers, AMG, 1992.

About the Author

Diane Junker was raised by parents who loved to study the Bible and passed on that love to her. For the past twenty-five years, she has taught and written Bible studies for groups at her church. Diane earned a bachelor's degree in biochemistry from the University of Wisconsin. She and her husband have two sons, a daughter-in-law, and three grandchildren.

Printed in the United States
by Baker & Taylor Publisher Services